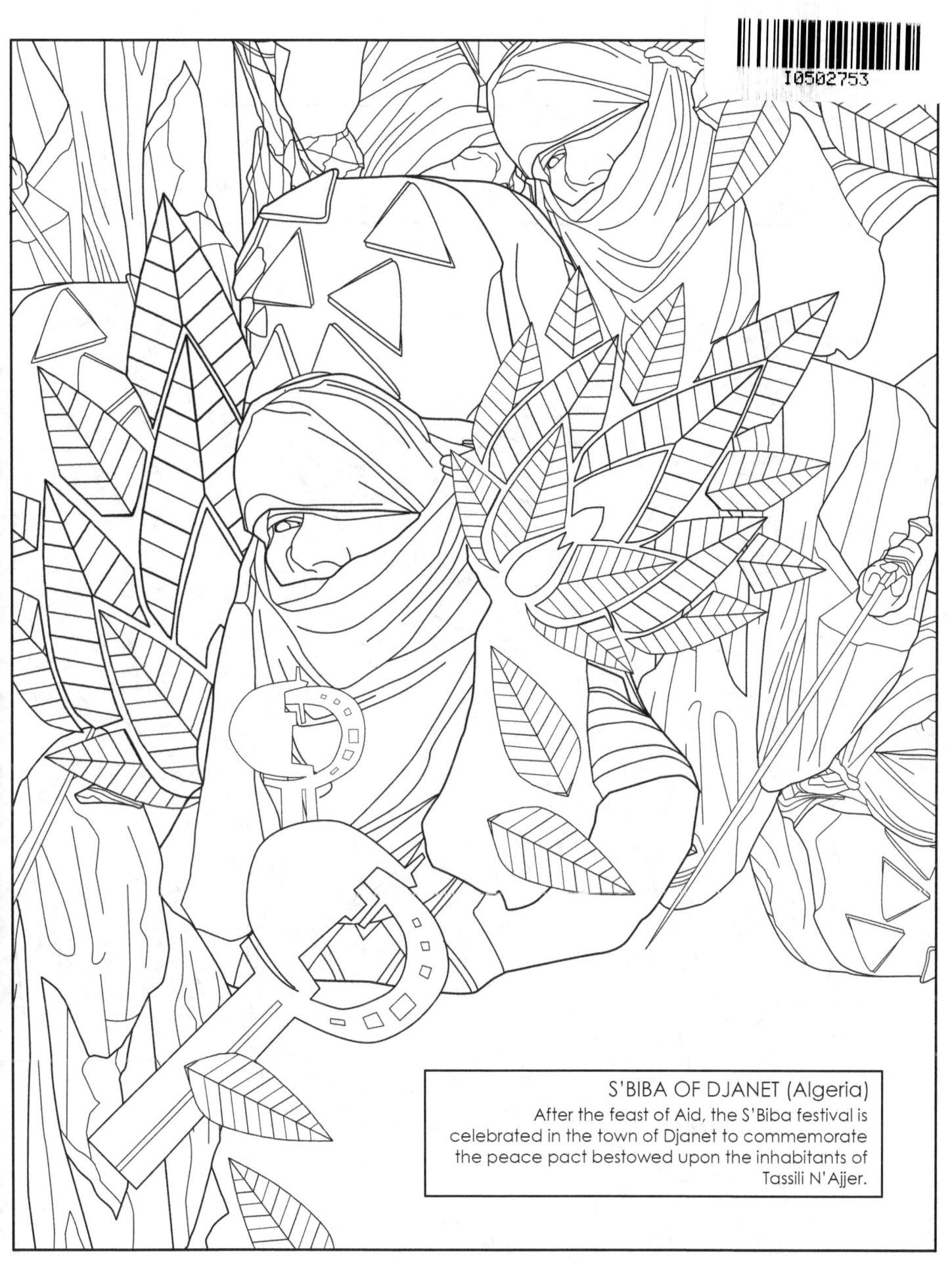

S'BIBA OF DJANET (Algeria)
After the feast of Aid, the S'Biba festival is celebrated in the town of Djanet to commemorate the peace pact bestowed upon the inhabitants of Tassili N'Ajjer.

GHADAMES INTERNATIONAL FESTIVAL (Libya)
Ghadames international festival is normally held in October, but dates can vary each year. In 2006, for example, the Festival was held in the month of November. It is a colourful event in which people gather to feast, sing and dance. A celebration of local Tuareg culture and traditions.

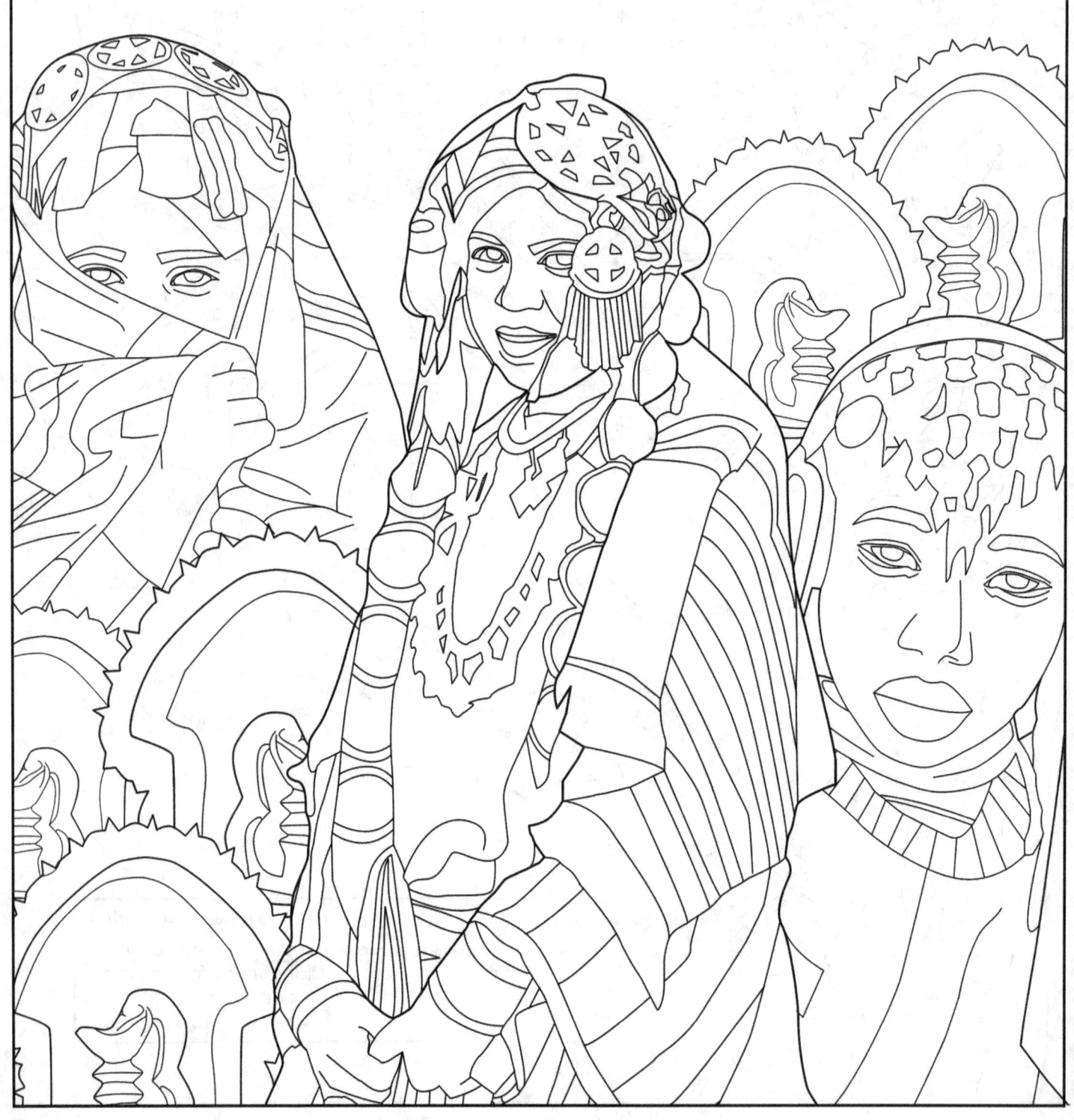

TIMITAR MUSIC FESTIVAL (Morocco)
Travel To Morocco For The Timitar Music Festival In Agadir featuring over 40 artists and 500,000 in attendance. Timitar Festival in Agadir, Morocco, has established itself as one the premiere African music festivals. Considered today as one of the biggest festivals in the country, Timitar provides its audience with an event well rooted in and actively working towards promoting Souss Massa Drâa culture.

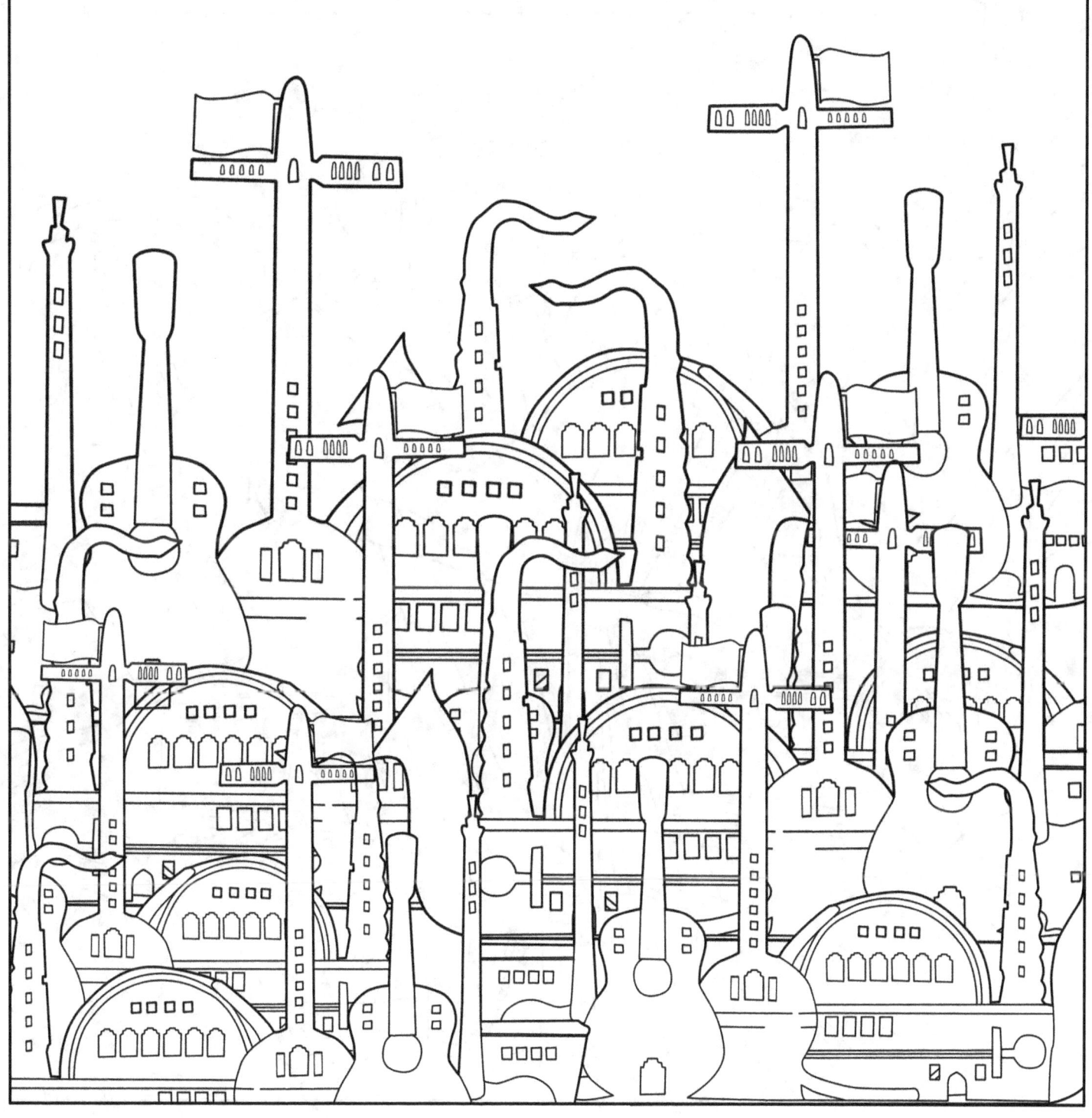

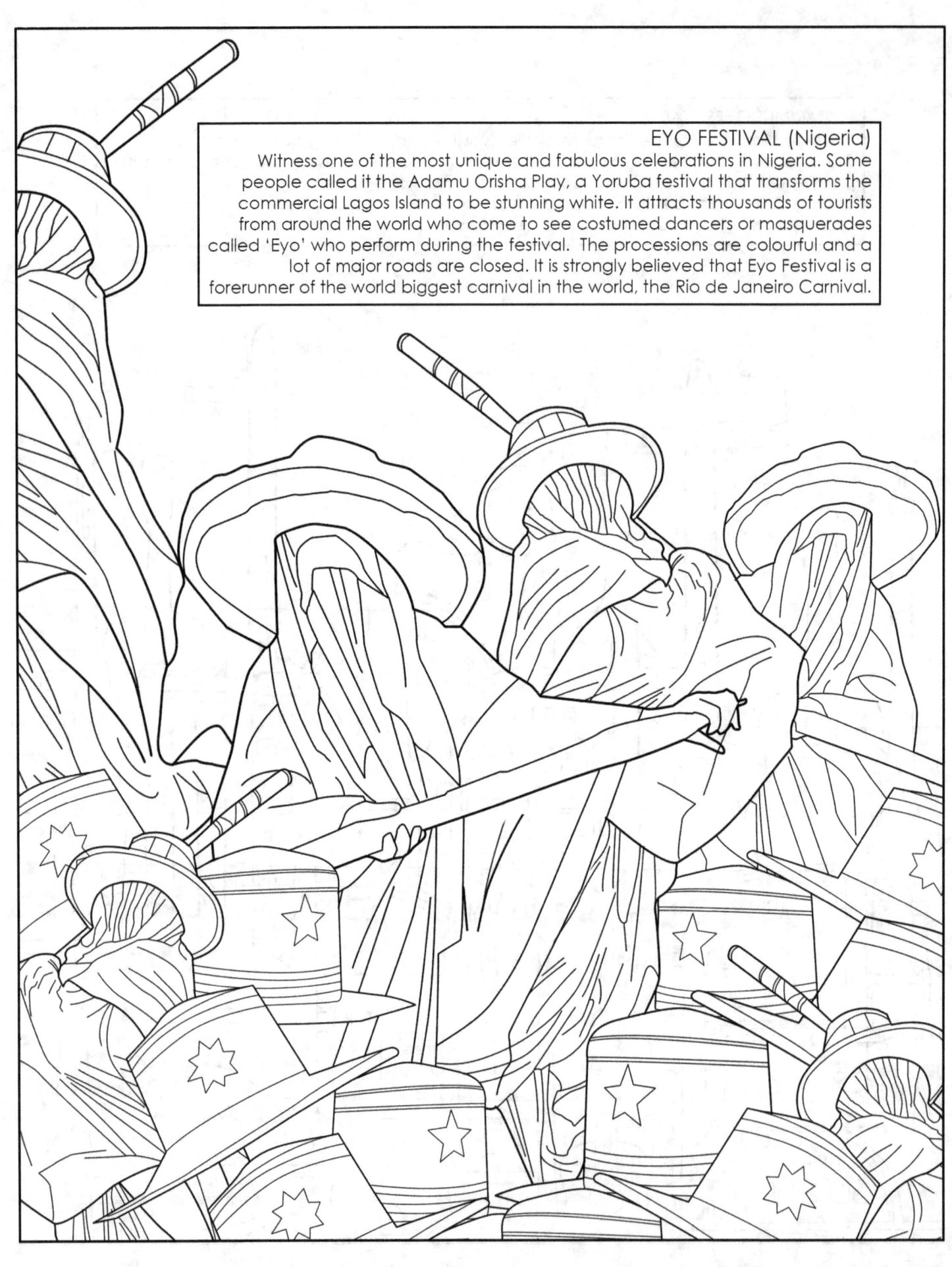

EYO FESTIVAL (Nigeria)
Witness one of the most unique and fabulous celebrations in Nigeria. Some people called it the Adamu Orisha Play, a Yoruba festival that transforms the commercial Lagos Island to be stunning white. It attracts thousands of tourists from around the world who come to see costumed dancers or masquerades called 'Eyo' who perform during the festival. The processions are colourful and a lot of major roads are closed. It is strongly believed that Eyo Festival is a forerunner of the world biggest carnival in the world, the Rio de Janeiro Carnival.

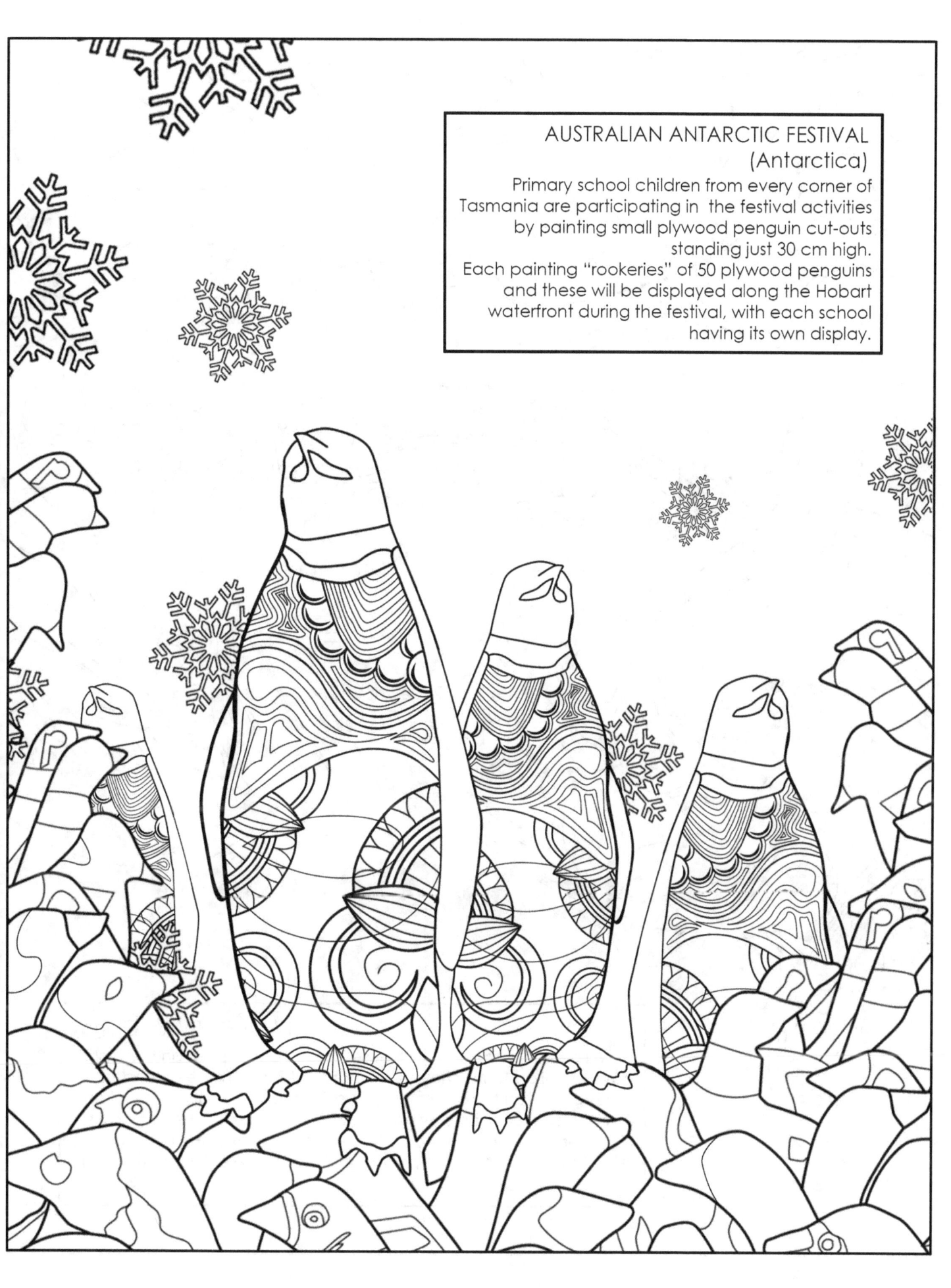

AUSTRALIAN ANTARCTIC FESTIVAL
(Antarctica)
Primary school children from every corner of
Tasmania are participating in the festival activities
by painting small plywood penguin cut-outs
standing just 30 cm high.
Each painting "rookeries" of 50 plywood penguins
and these will be displayed along the Hobart
waterfront during the festival, with each school
having its own display.

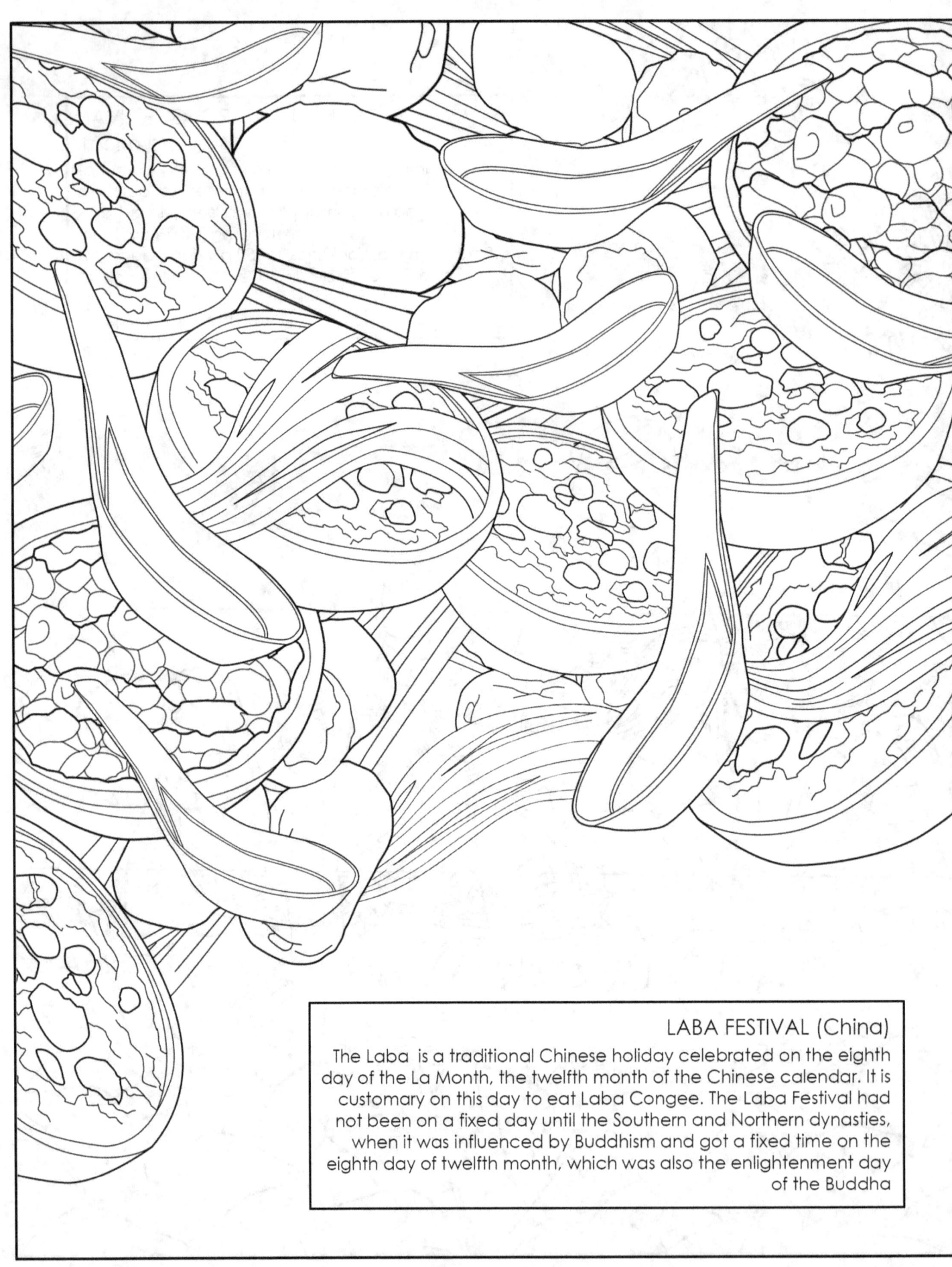

LABA FESTIVAL (China)

The Laba is a traditional Chinese holiday celebrated on the eighth day of the La Month, the twelfth month of the Chinese calendar. It is customary on this day to eat Laba Congee. The Laba Festival had not been on a fixed day until the Southern and Northern dynasties, when it was influenced by Buddhism and got a fixed time on the eighth day of twelfth month, which was also the enlightenment day of the Buddha

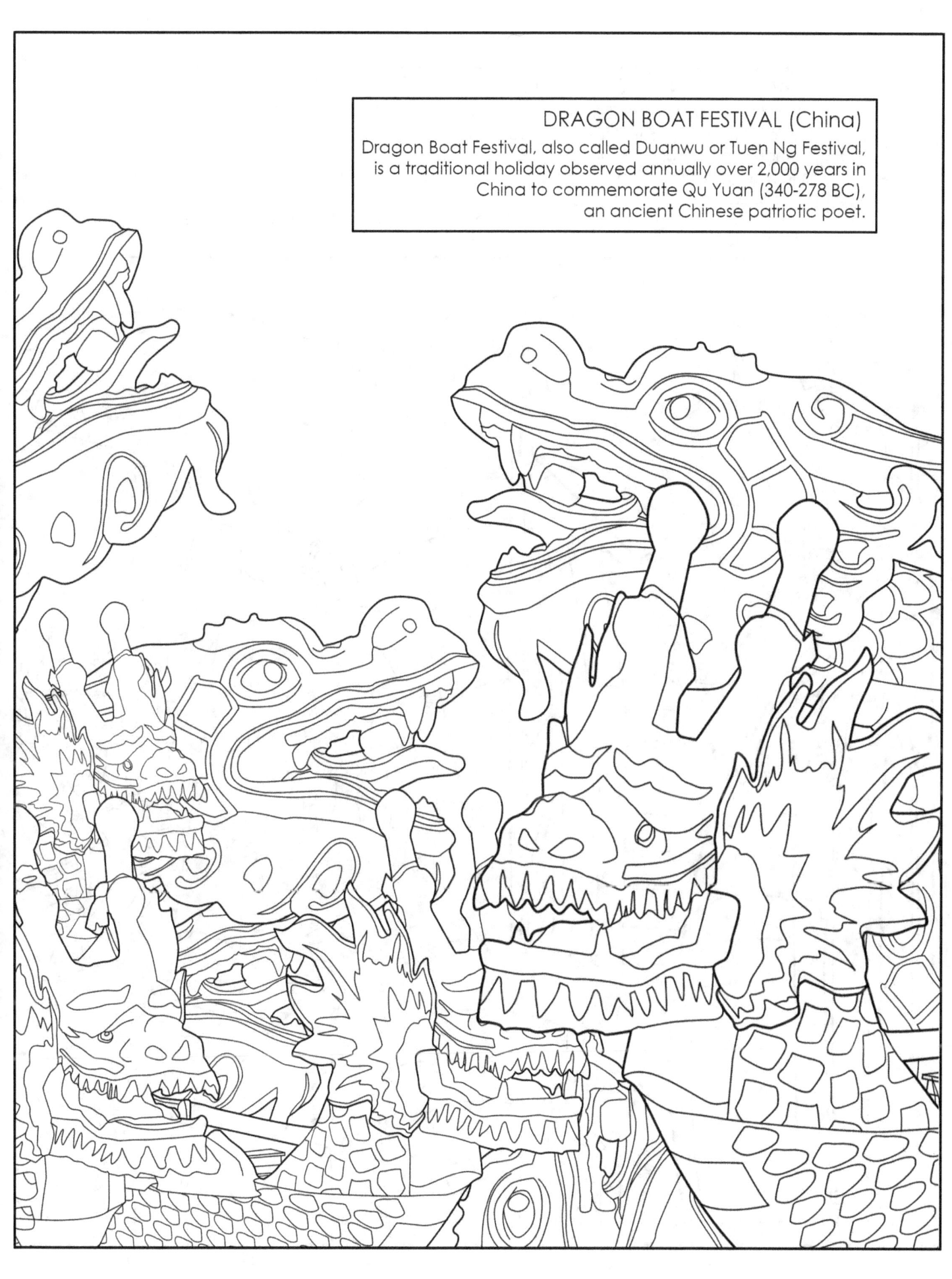

DRAGON BOAT FESTIVAL (China)
Dragon Boat Festival, also called Duanwu or Tuen Ng Festival, is a traditional holiday observed annually over 2,000 years in China to commemorate Qu Yuan (340-278 BC), an ancient Chinese patriotic poet.

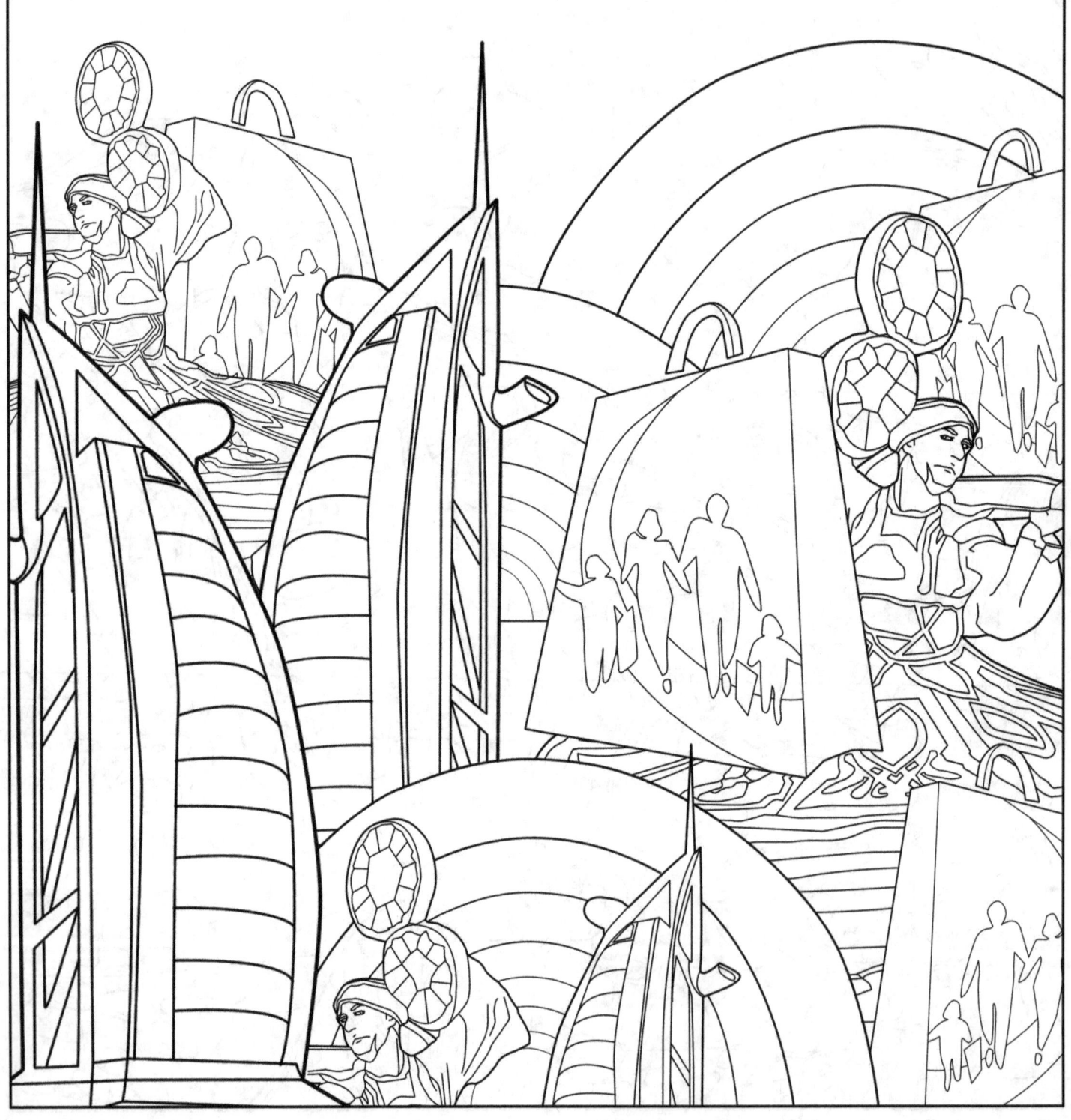

DUBAI SHOPPING FESTIVAL (Dubai)
Dubai Shopping Festival (DSF) started on 16 February 1996 as a retail event intended to benefit retail trade in Dubai, United Arab Emirates. It has since been promoted as a tourist attraction.[citation needed] It is an annual month-long event, usually scheduled during the first quarter of the year, and attracts about 3 million people to Dubai.
During the Festival, shops offer discounts on their merchandise, daily car raffles are drawn, and there is a fireworks display.

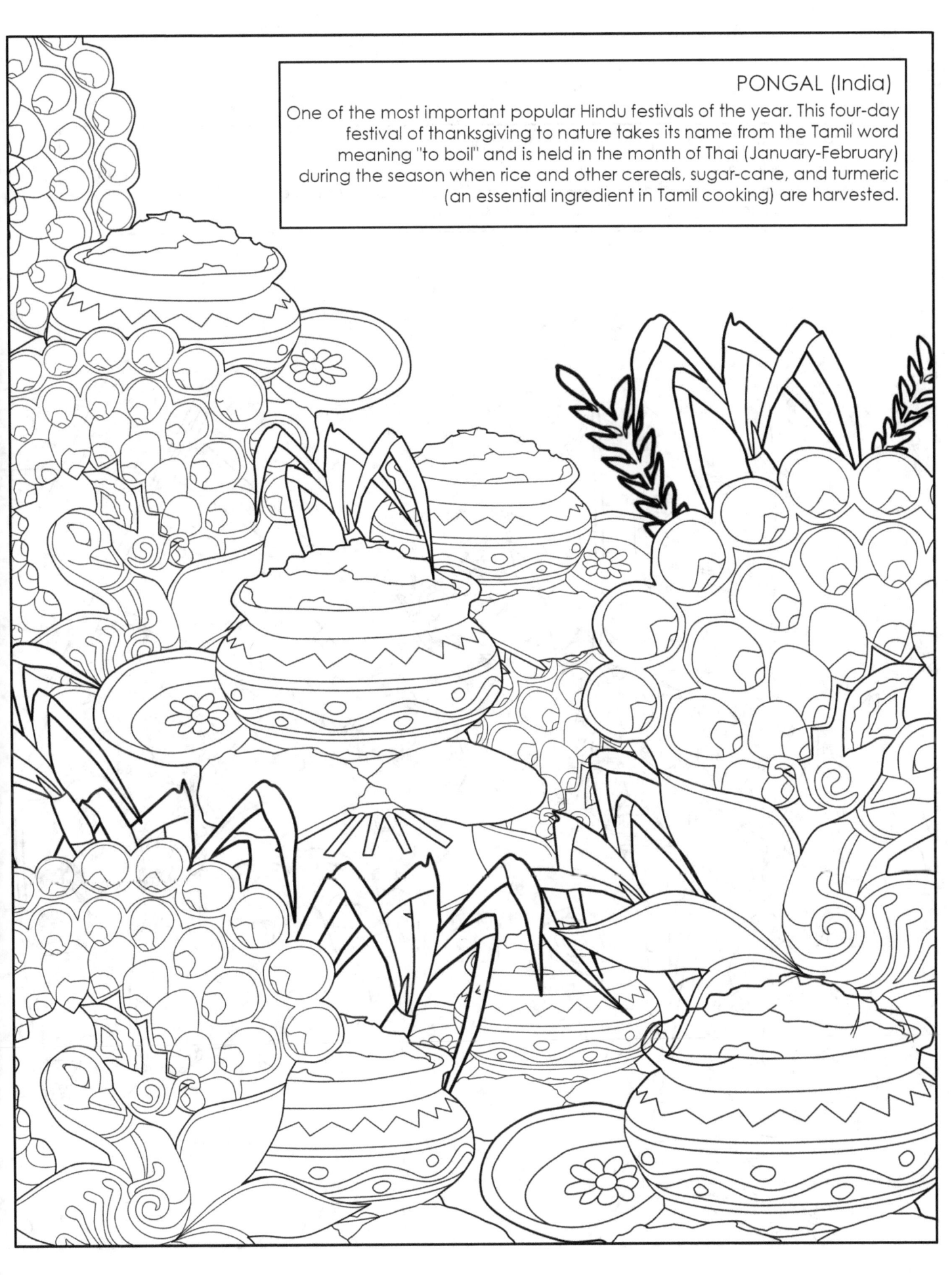

PONGAL (India)
One of the most important popular Hindu festivals of the year. This four-day festival of thanksgiving to nature takes its name from the Tamil word meaning "to boil" and is held in the month of Thai (January-February) during the season when rice and other cereals, sugar-cane, and turmeric (an essential ingredient in Tamil cooking) are harvested.

INTERNATIONAL PUPPET FESTIVAL (Istanbul)

International Istanbul Puppet Festival — This now almost forgotten art was once big in Ottoman times. A great chance to catch puppet, marionette and shadow theater. Most plays are silent, so suitable for children and adults. (2nd week of May, small venues all over town)

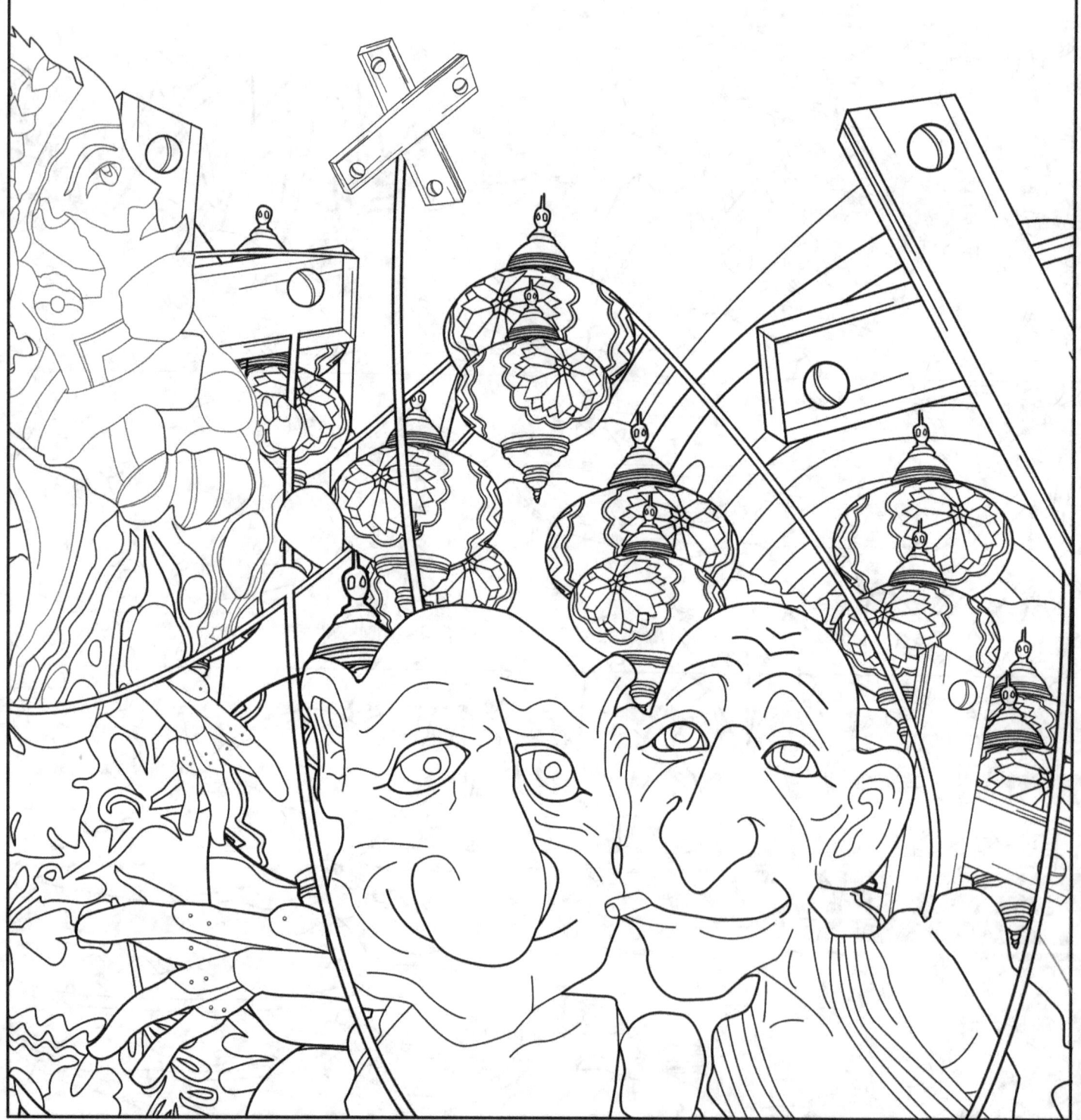

OBON FESTIVAL (Japan)

Obon is a Japanese Buddhist custom to honor the spirits of one's ancestors. This Buddhist-Confucian custom has evolved into a family reunion holiday during which people return to ancestral family places and visit and clean their ancestors' graves, and when the spirits of ancestors are supposed to revisit the household altars. It has been celebrated in Japan for more than 500 years and traditionally includes a dance, known as Bon-Odori.

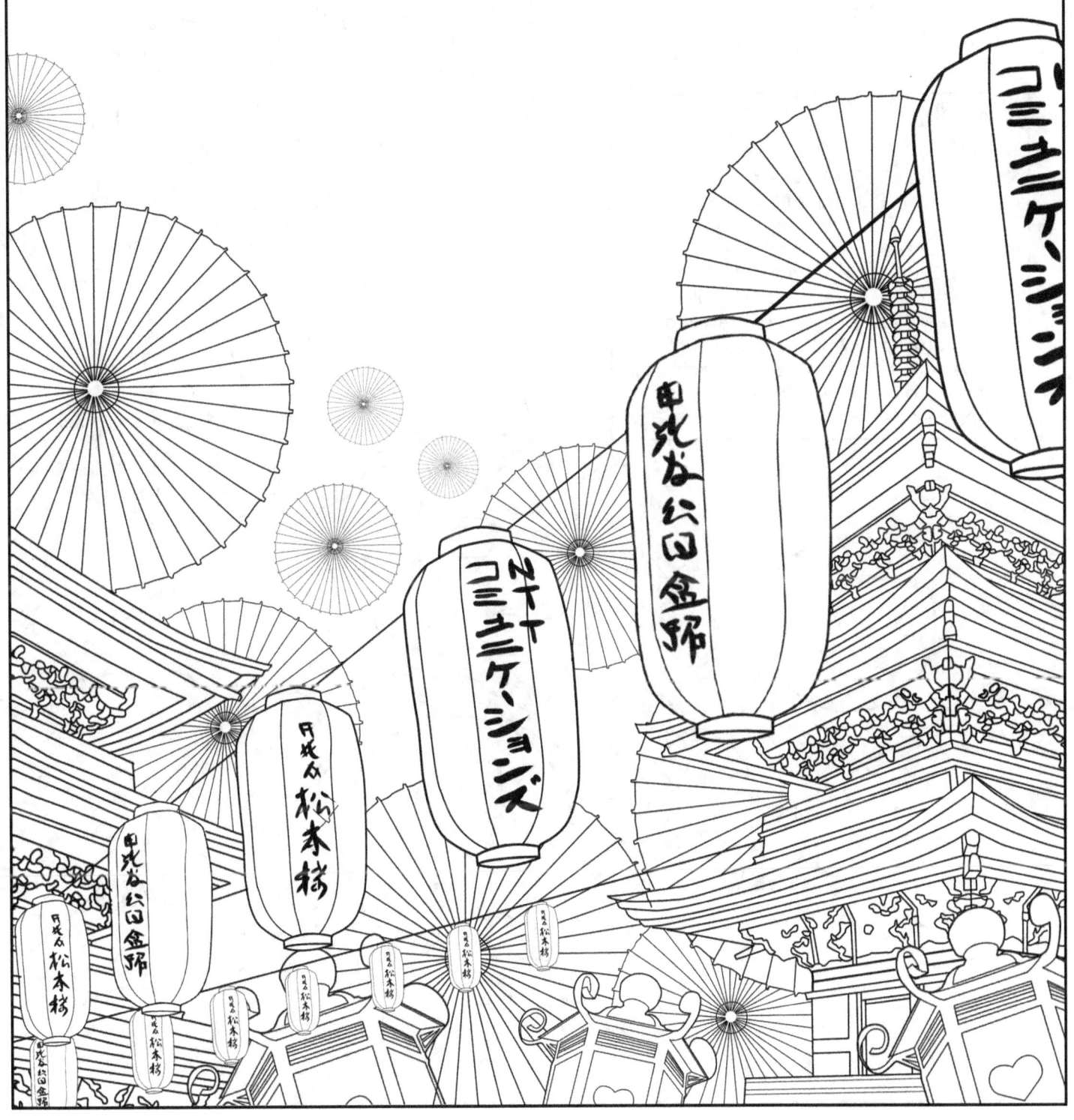

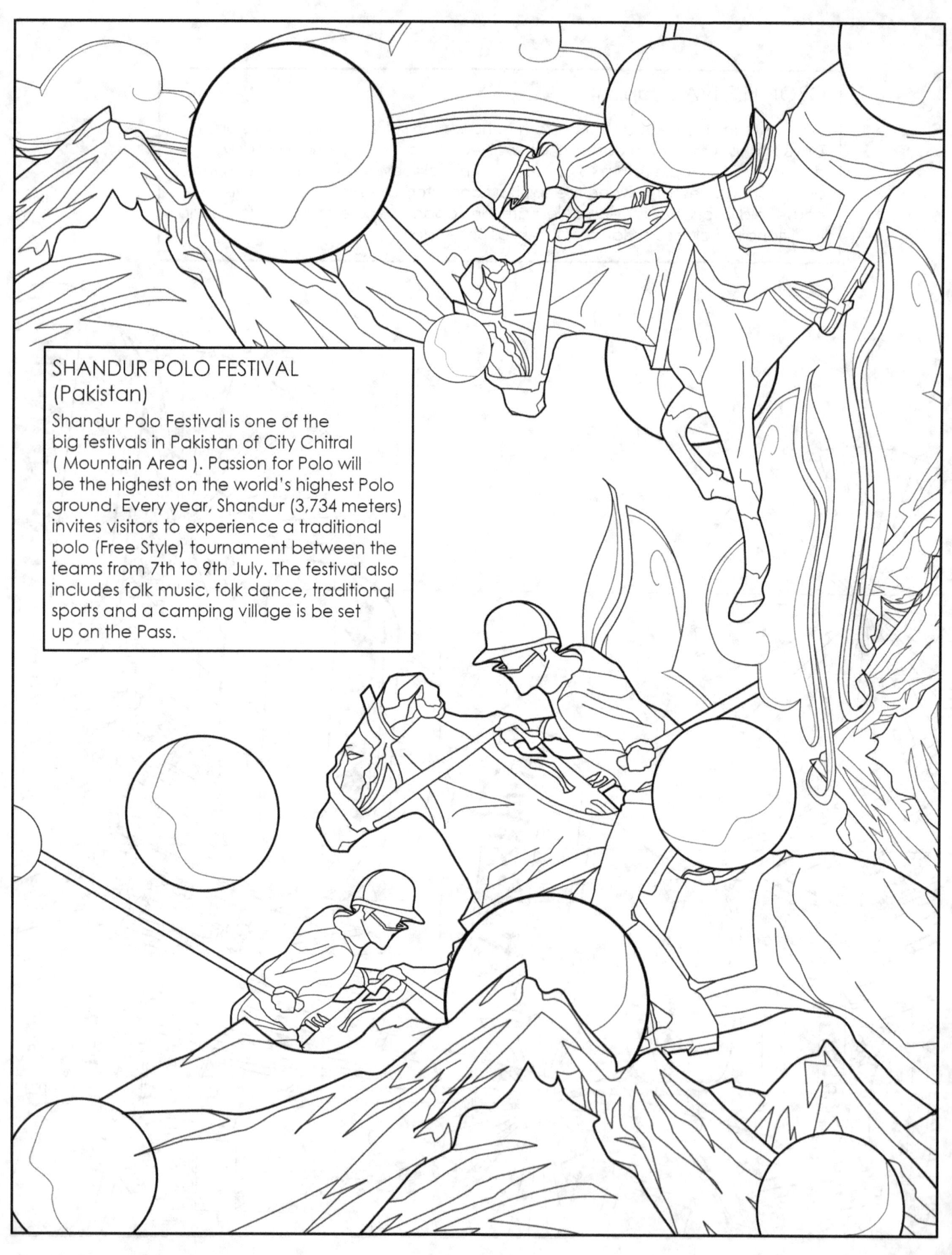

SHANDUR POLO FESTIVAL
(Pakistan)
Shandur Polo Festival is one of the
big festivals in Pakistan of City Chitral
(Mountain Area). Passion for Polo will
be the highest on the world's highest Polo
ground. Every year, Shandur (3,734 meters)
invites visitors to experience a traditional
polo (Free Style) tournament between the
teams from 7th to 9th July. The festival also
includes folk music, folk dance, traditional
sports and a camping village is be set
up on the Pass.

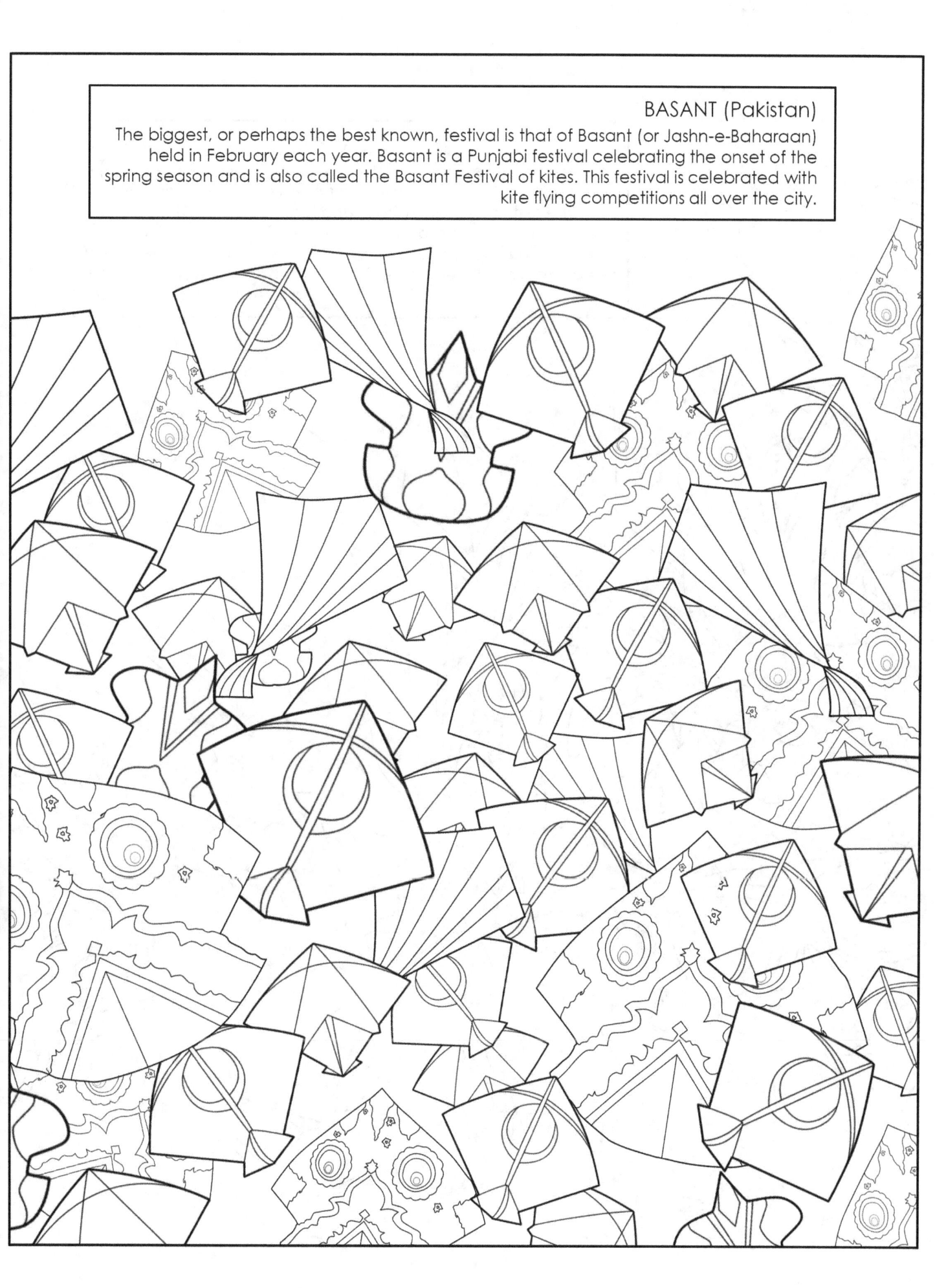

BASANT (Pakistan)

The biggest, or perhaps the best known, festival is that of Basant (or Jashn-e-Baharaan) held in February each year. Basant is a Punjabi festival celebrating the onset of the spring season and is also called the Basant Festival of kites. This festival is celebrated with kite flying competitions all over the city.

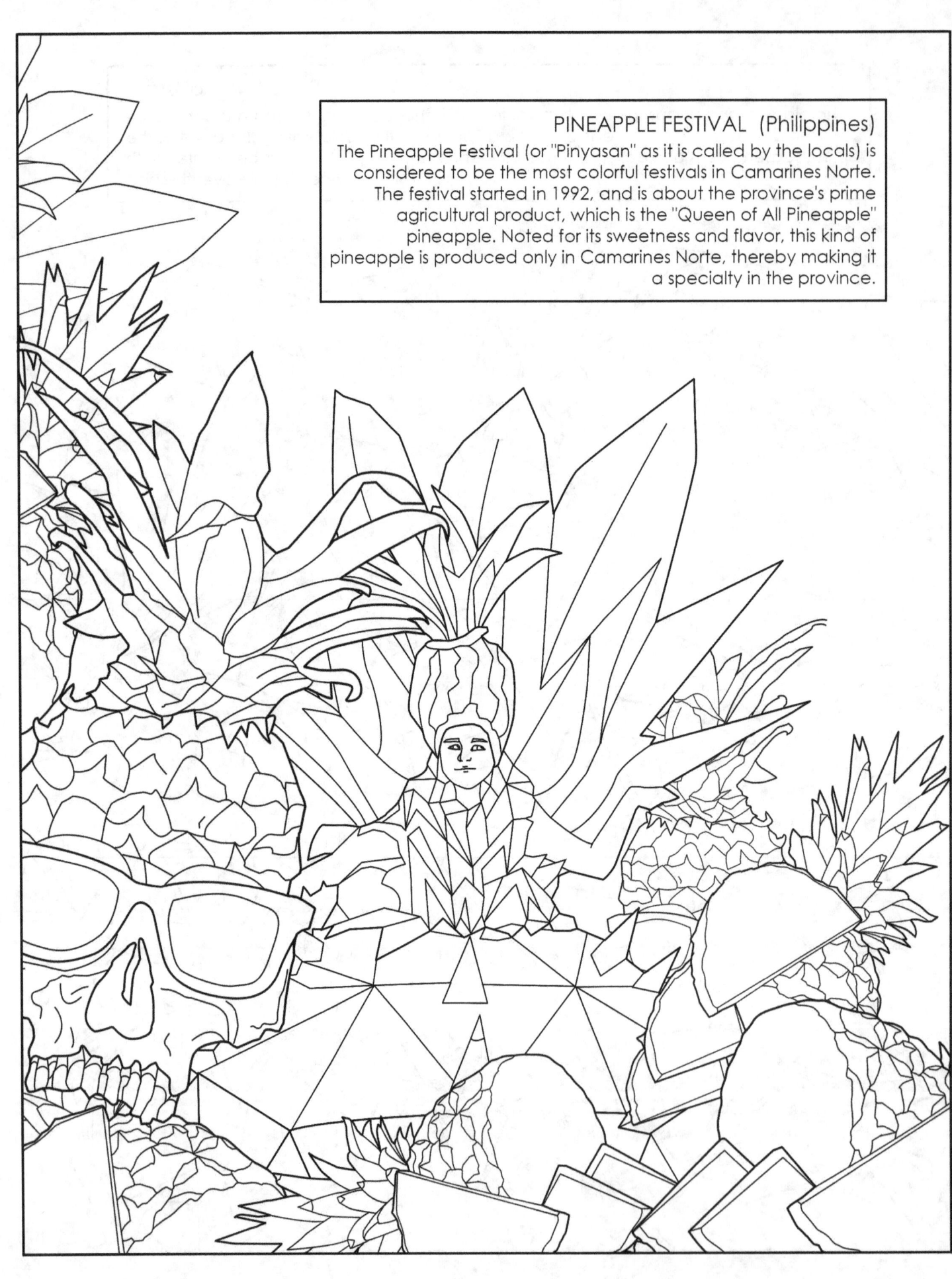

PINEAPPLE FESTIVAL (Philippines)
The Pineapple Festival (or "Pinyasan" as it is called by the locals) is considered to be the most colorful festivals in Camarines Norte. The festival started in 1992, and is about the province's prime agricultural product, which is the "Queen of All Pineapple" pineapple. Noted for its sweetness and flavor, this kind of pineapple is produced only in Camarines Norte, thereby making it a specialty in the province.

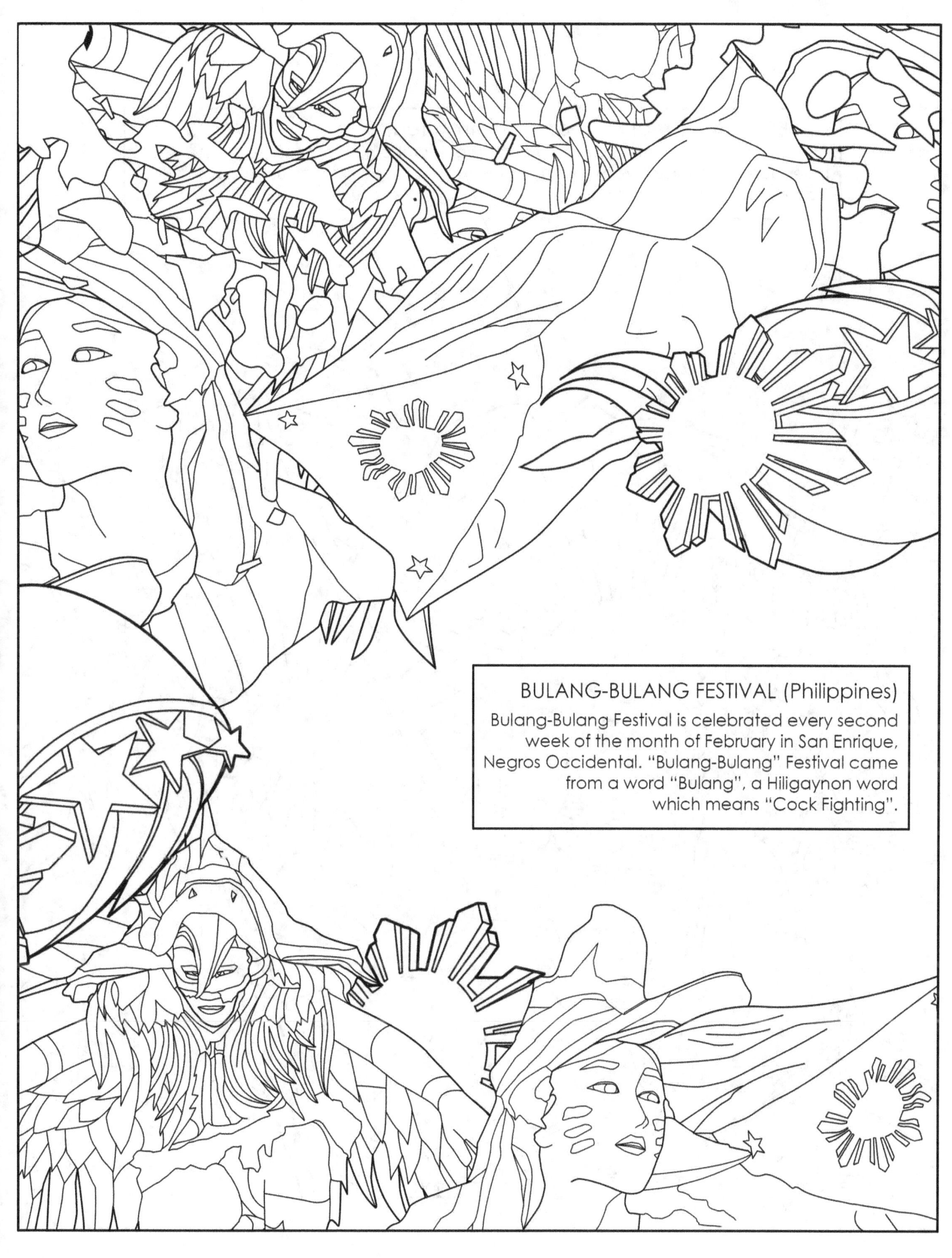

BULANG-BULANG FESTIVAL (Philippines)
Bulang-Bulang Festival is celebrated every second week of the month of February in San Enrique, Negros Occidental. "Bulang-Bulang" Festival came from a word "Bulang", a Hiligaynon word which means "Cock Fighting".

DAEBOREUM "Great Full Moon" (South Korea)
Korean holiday that celebrates the first full moon of the new year of the lunar Korean
calendar which is the Korean version of the First Full Moon Festival. This holiday is
accompanied by many trditions.

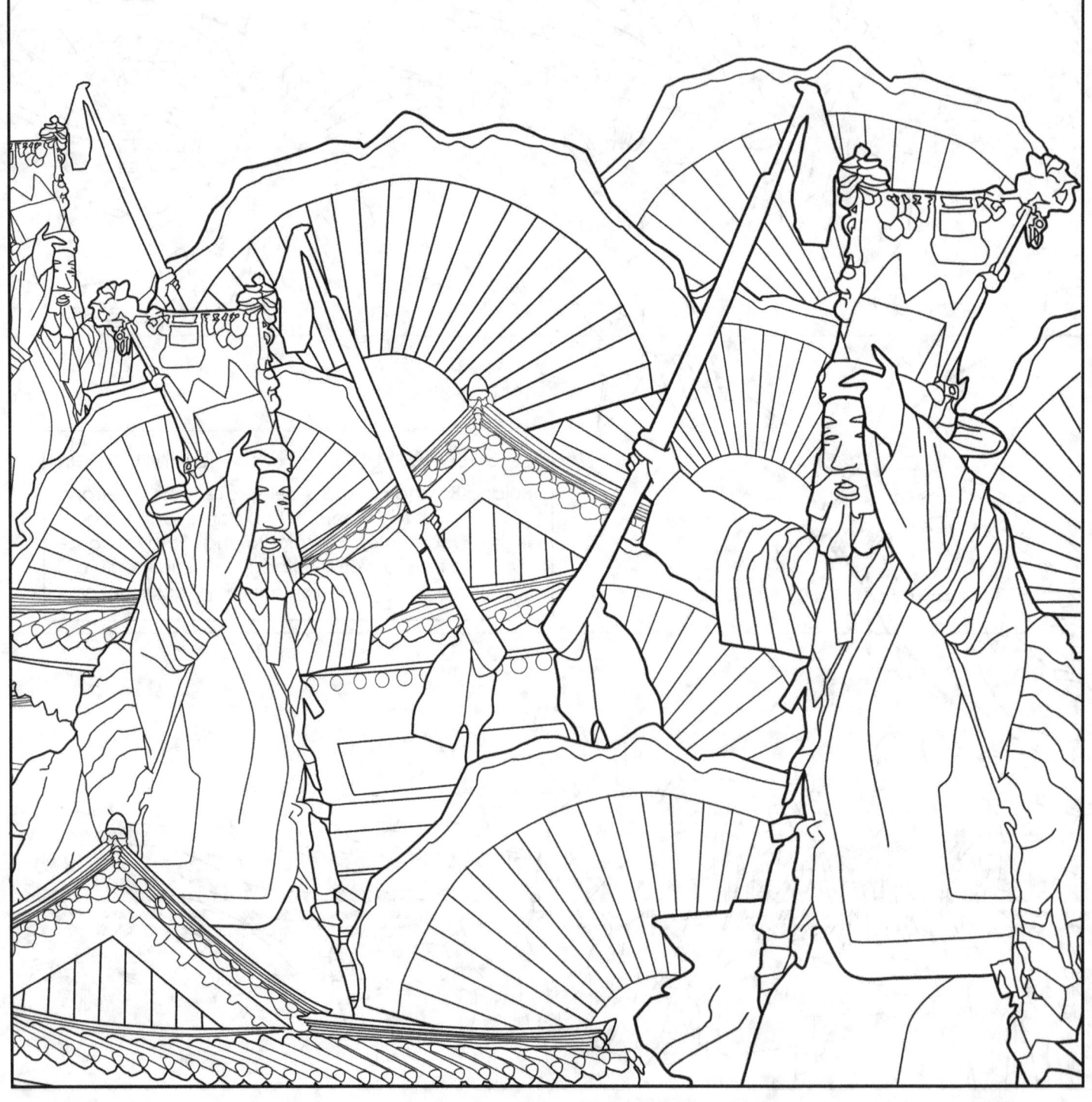

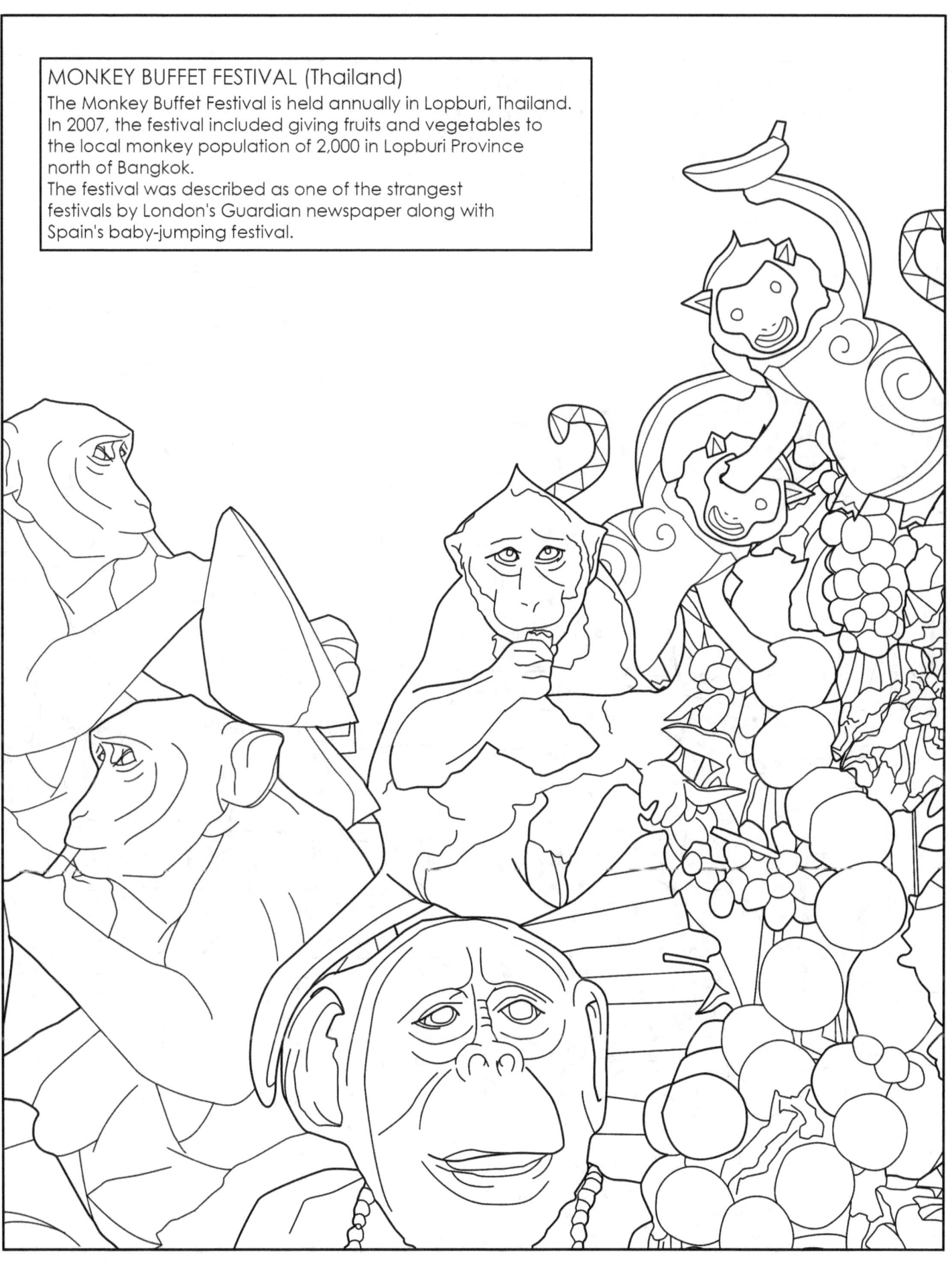

MONKEY BUFFET FESTIVAL (Thailand)
The Monkey Buffet Festival is held annually in Lopburi, Thailand.
In 2007, the festival included giving fruits and vegetables to
the local monkey population of 2,000 in Lopburi Province
north of Bangkok.
The festival was described as one of the strangest
festivals by London's Guardian newspaper along with
Spain's baby-jumping festival.

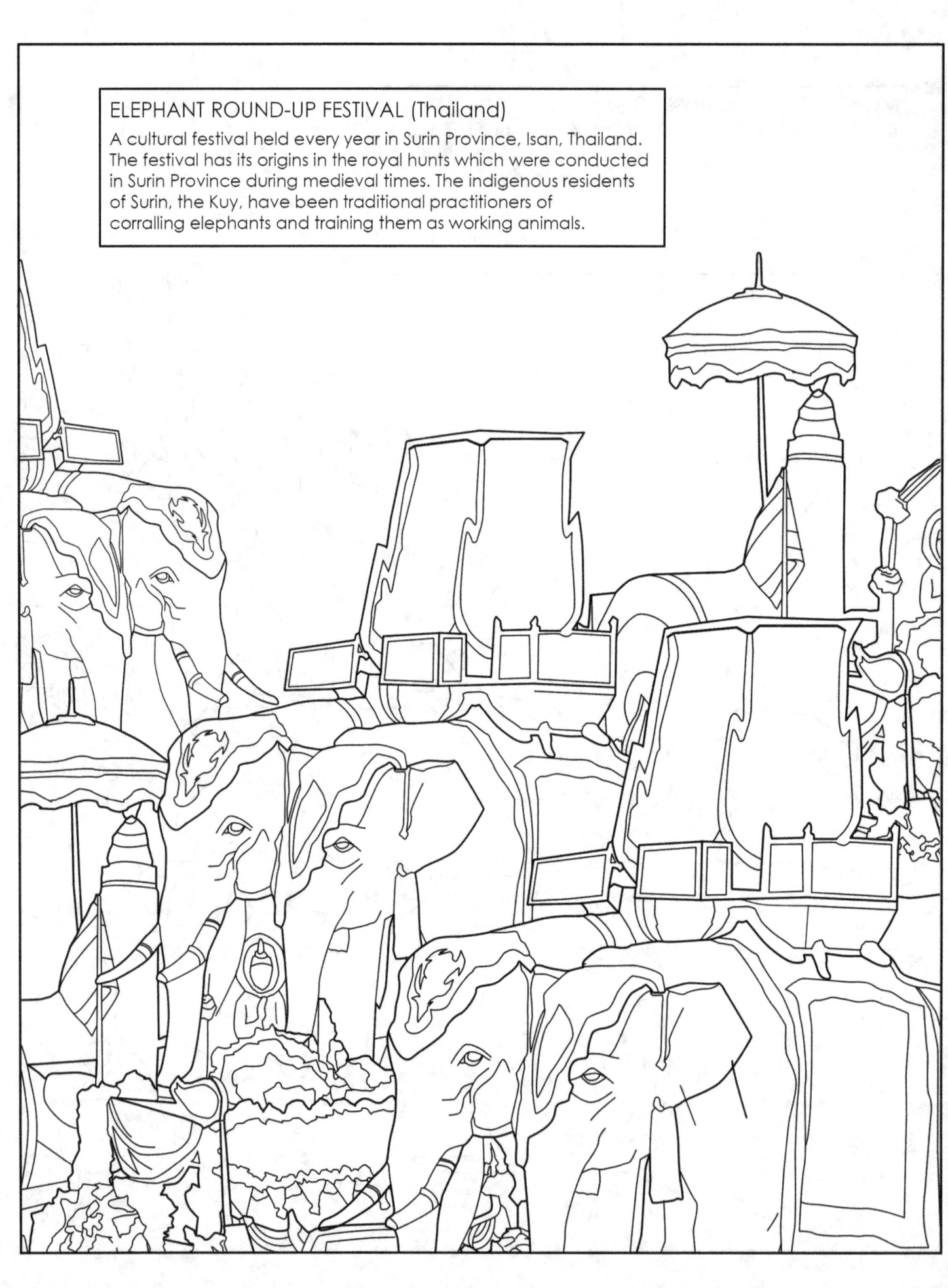

ELEPHANT ROUND-UP FESTIVAL (Thailand)

A cultural festival held every year in Surin Province, Isan, Thailand. The festival has its origins in the royal hunts which were conducted in Surin Province during medieval times. The indigenous residents of Surin, the Kuy, have been traditional practitioners of corralling elephants and training them as working animals.

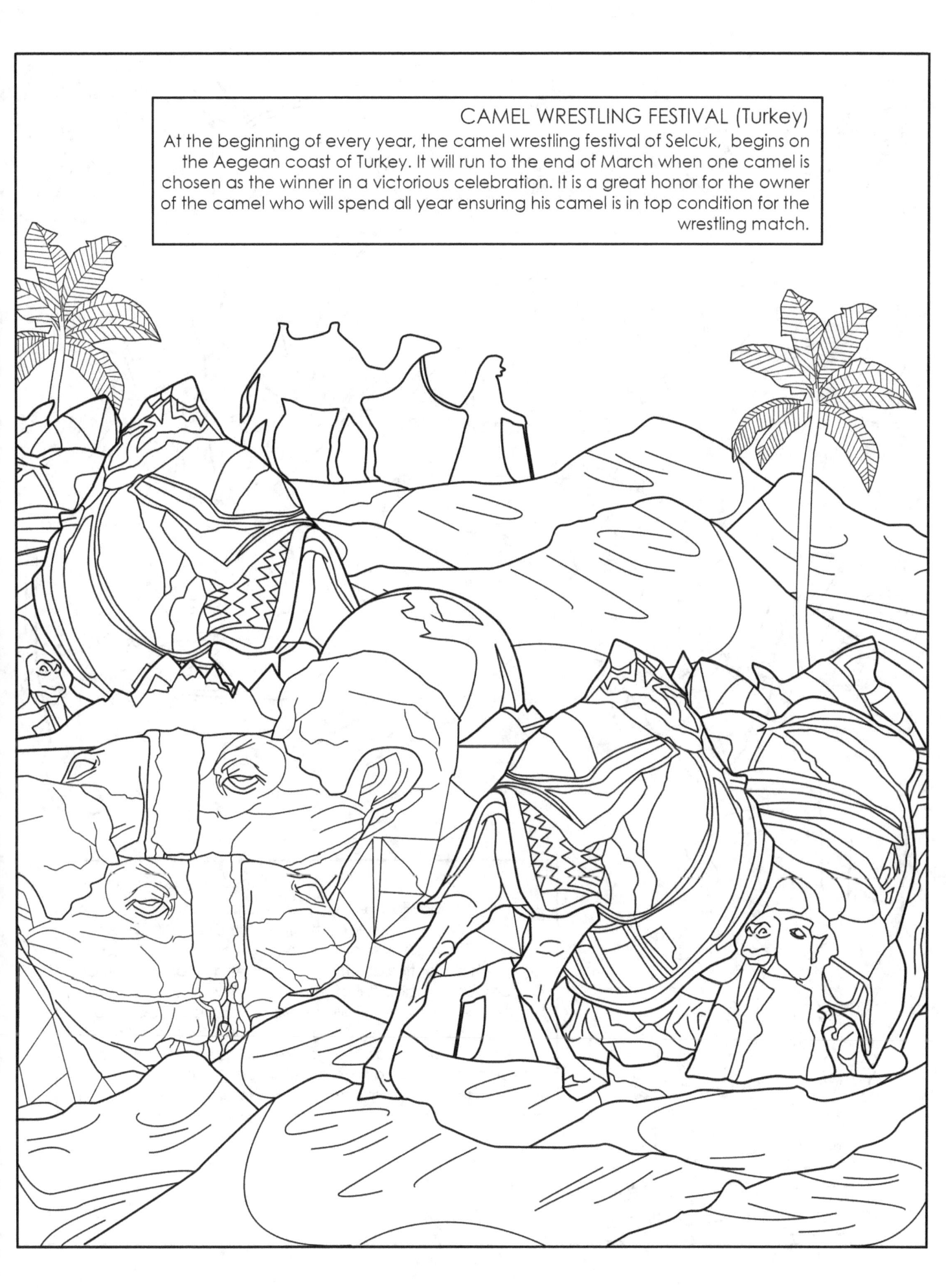

CAMEL WRESTLING FESTIVAL (Turkey)
At the beginning of every year, the camel wrestling festival of Selcuk, begins on the Aegean coast of Turkey. It will run to the end of March when one camel is chosen as the winner in a victorious celebration. It is a great honor for the owner of the camel who will spend all year ensuring his camel is in top condition for the wrestling match.

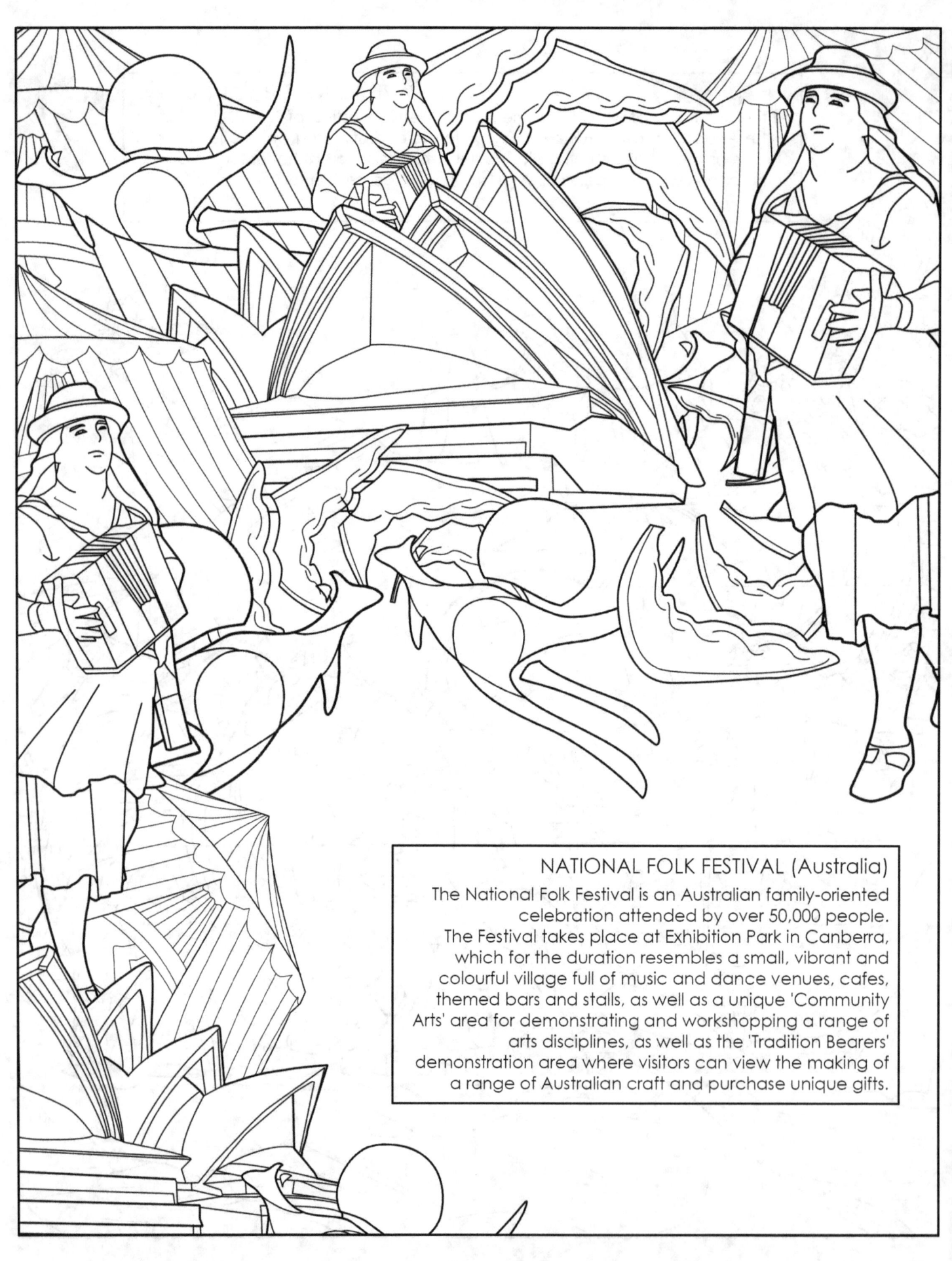

NATIONAL FOLK FESTIVAL (Australia)

The National Folk Festival is an Australian family-oriented celebration attended by over 50,000 people. The Festival takes place at Exhibition Park in Canberra, which for the duration resembles a small, vibrant and colourful village full of music and dance venues, cafes, themed bars and stalls, as well as a unique 'Community Arts' area for demonstrating and workshopping a range of arts disciplines, as well as the 'Tradition Bearers' demonstration area where visitors can view the making of a range of Australian craft and purchase unique gifts.

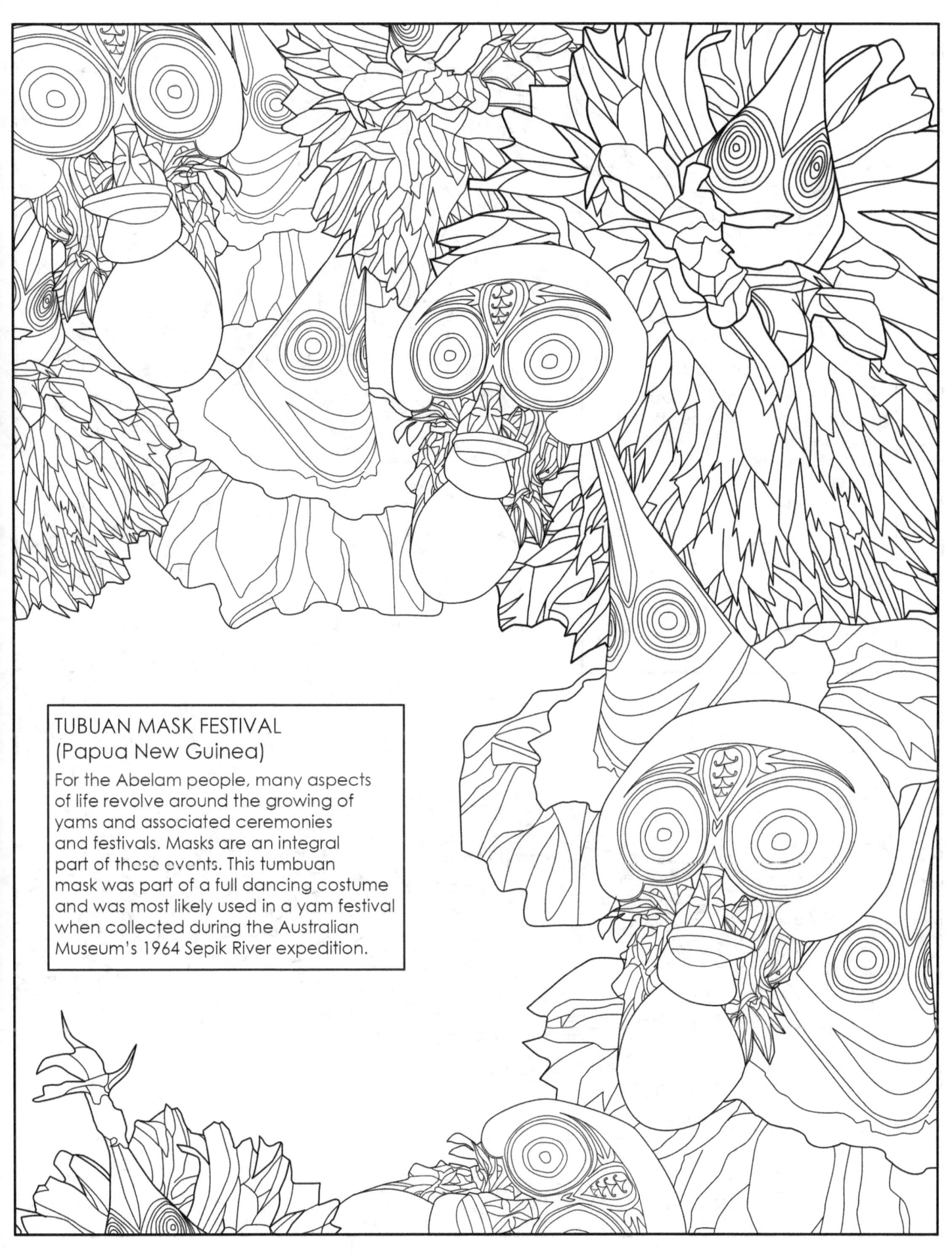

TUBUAN MASK FESTIVAL
(Papua New Guinea)

For the Abelam people, many aspects of life revolve around the growing of yams and associated ceremonies and festivals. Masks are an integral part of these events. This tumbuan mask was part of a full dancing costume and was most likely used in a yam festival when collected during the Australian Museum's 1964 Sepik River expedition.

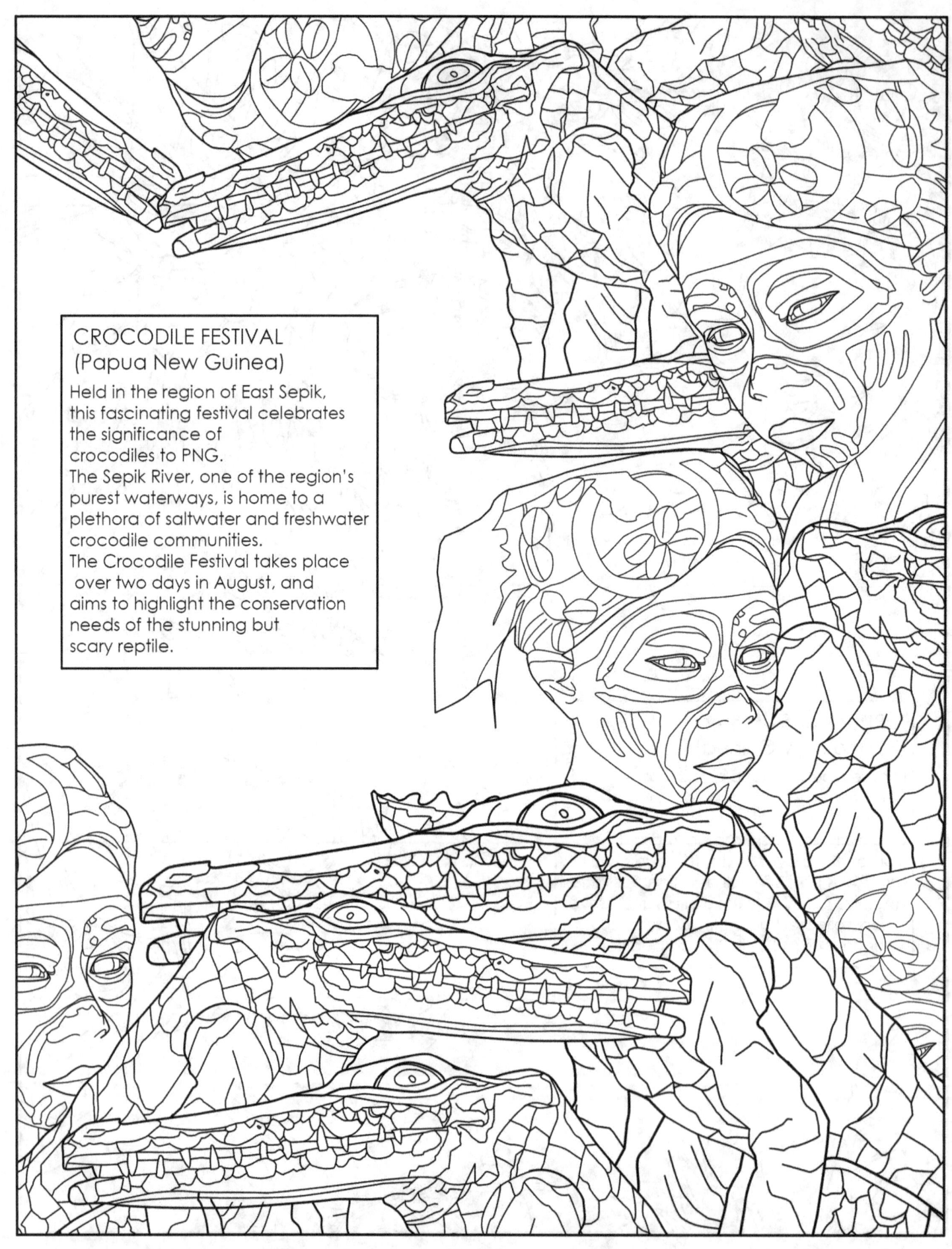

CROCODILE FESTIVAL
(Papua New Guinea)

Held in the region of East Sepik,
this fascinating festival celebrates
the significance of
crocodiles to PNG.
The Sepik River, one of the region's
purest waterways, is home to a
plethora of saltwater and freshwater
crocodile communities.
The Crocodile Festival takes place
over two days in August, and
aims to highlight the conservation
needs of the stunning but
scary reptile.

WORLD BODYPAINTING FESTIVAL (Austria)

The World Bodypainting Festival (abbreviated WBF) is an annual bodypainting festival and competition held in Pörtschach, Austria on lake Wörthersee.

The festival was first created and launched in 1998 in Seeboden, Austria as the European Bodypainting Festival in order to promote summer tourism to the region by then tourism manager Alex Barendregt. It was a small gathering of artists and the first "boutique event" of its kind in the world. Also launched in conjunction was the WB Academy, which in 2008 was offered worldwide. As the Bodypainting Movement was growing, in 2001 Mr. Barendregt launched the WB Association followed by the launch of the WB Production in 2010.

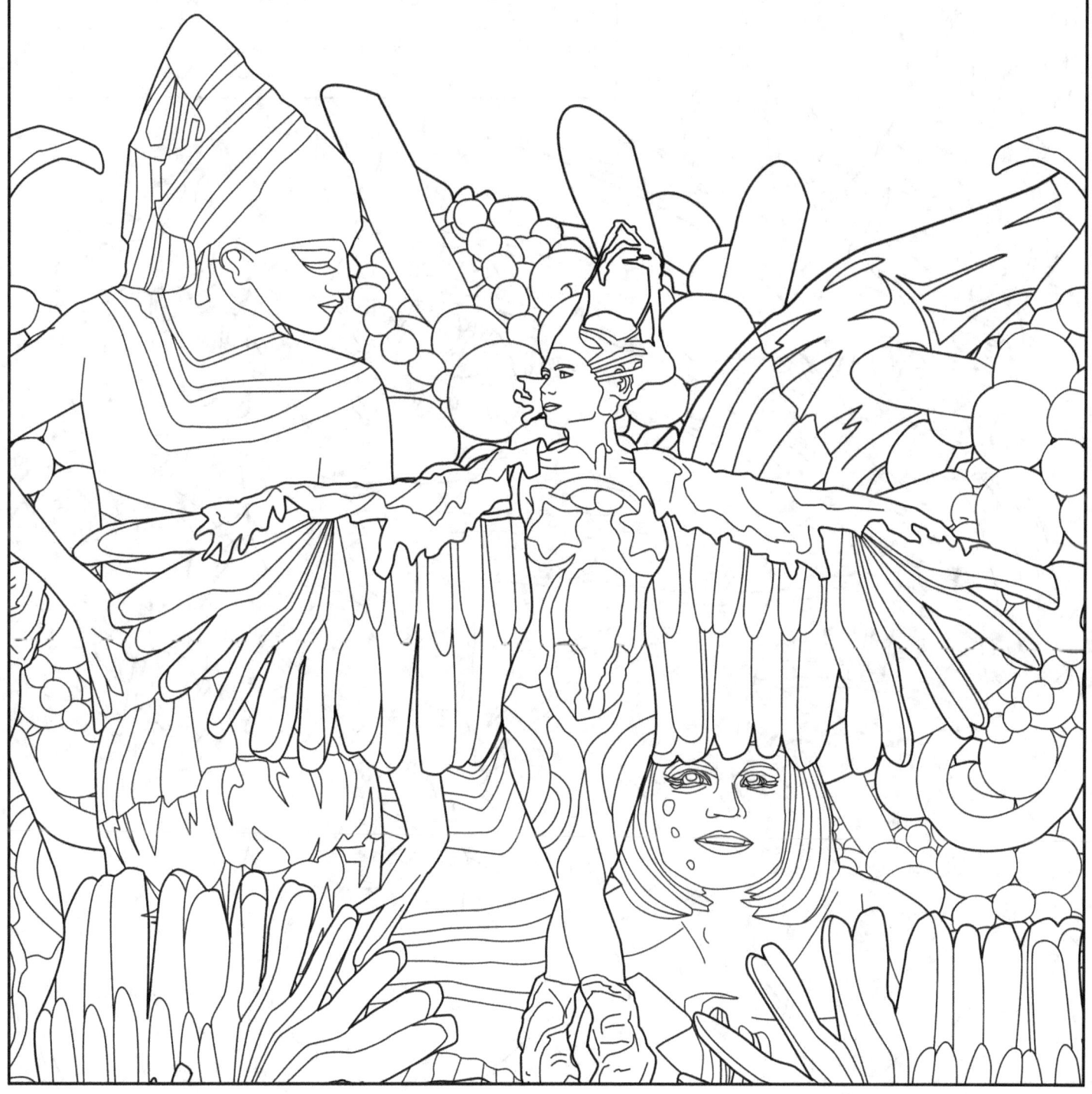

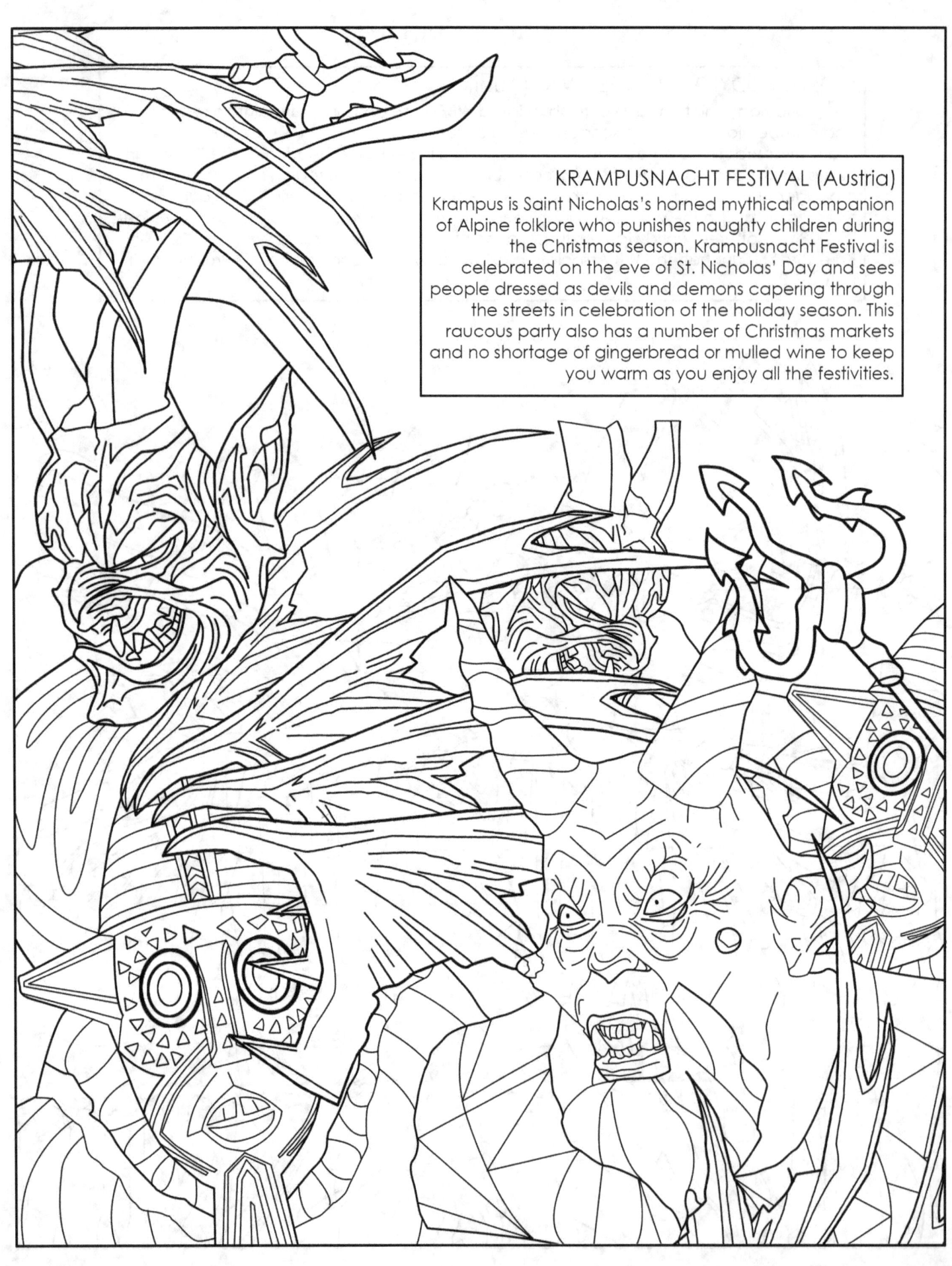

KRAMPUSNACHT FESTIVAL (Austria)

Krampus is Saint Nicholas's horned mythical companion of Alpine folklore who punishes naughty children during the Christmas season. Krampusnacht Festival is celebrated on the eve of St. Nicholas' Day and sees people dressed as devils and demons capering through the streets in celebration of the holiday season. This raucous party also has a number of Christmas markets and no shortage of gingerbread or mulled wine to keep you warm as you enjoy all the festivities.

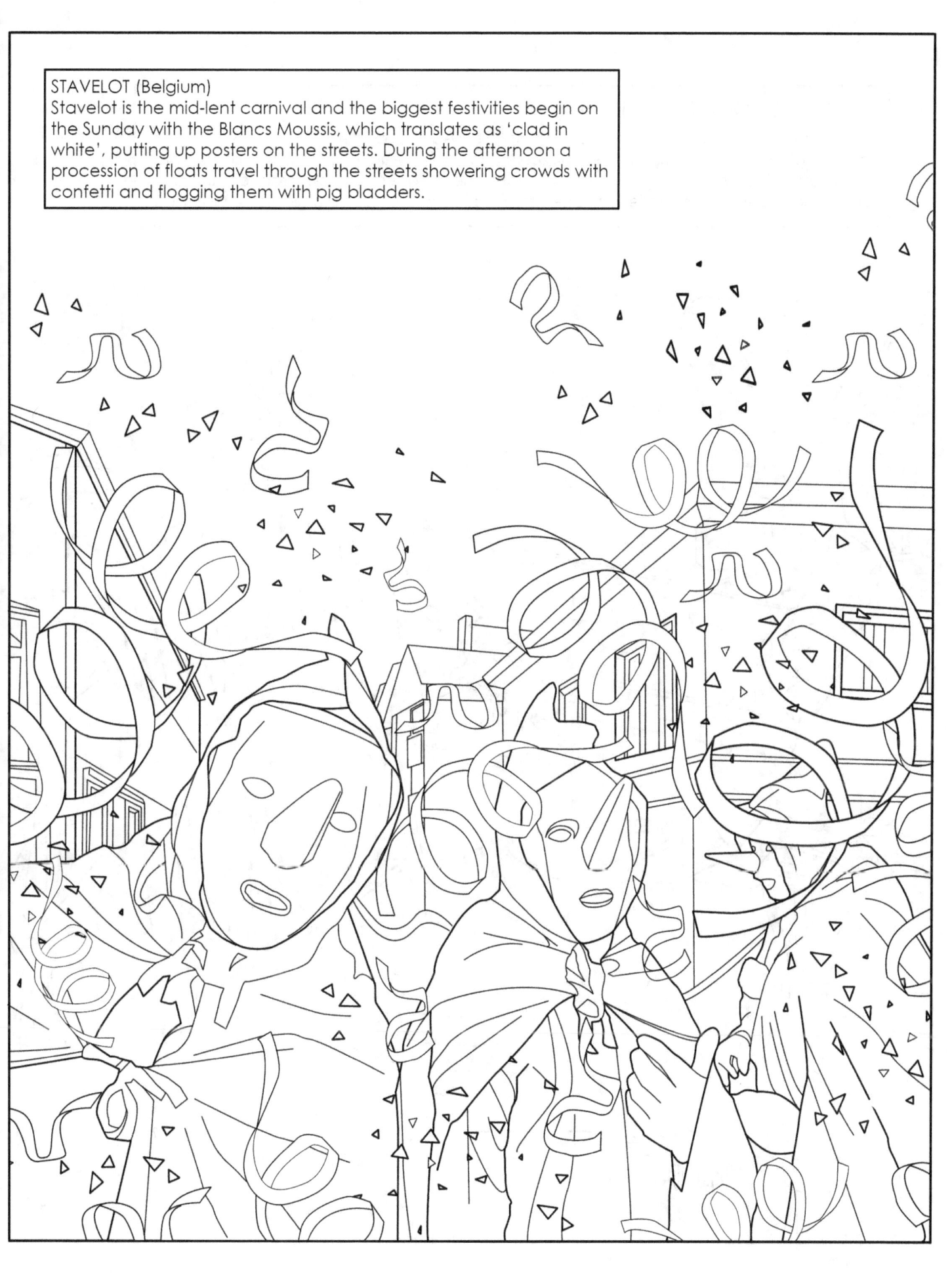

STAVELOT (Belgium)
Stavelot is the mid-lent carnival and the biggest festivities begin on the Sunday with the Blancs Moussis, which translates as 'clad in white', putting up posters on the streets. During the afternoon a procession of floats travel through the streets showering crowds with confetti and flogging them with pig bladders.

Always held on the fourth weekend of August, this medieval pageant celebrates the wedding of Monsieur and Madame Gouyasse (Goliath). The festival includes a ceremony at Saint Julian's church, after which Goliath fights the shepherd David in front of the town hall. During the Sunday parade, onlookers throw coins at the dancing giants for good luck.

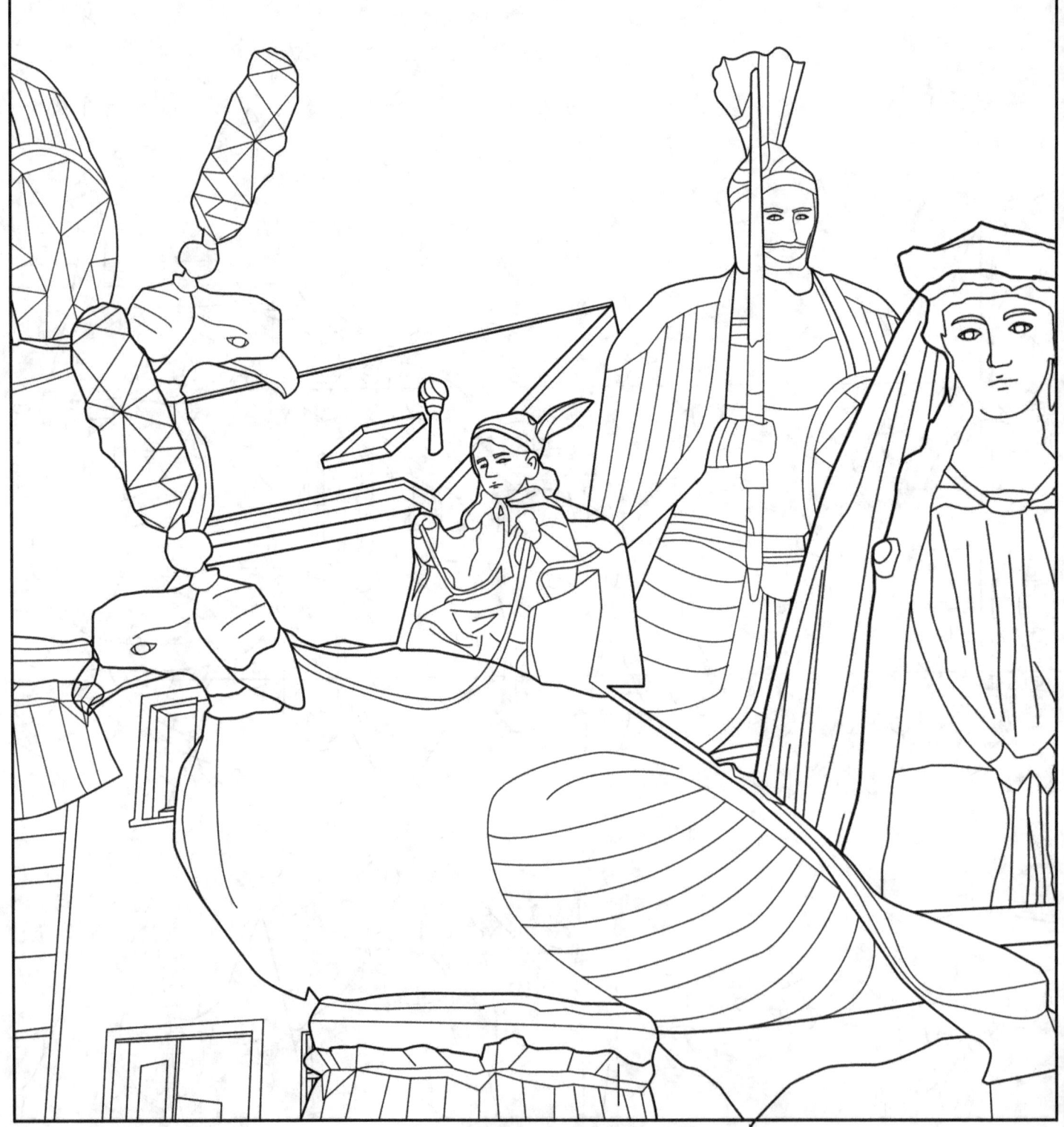

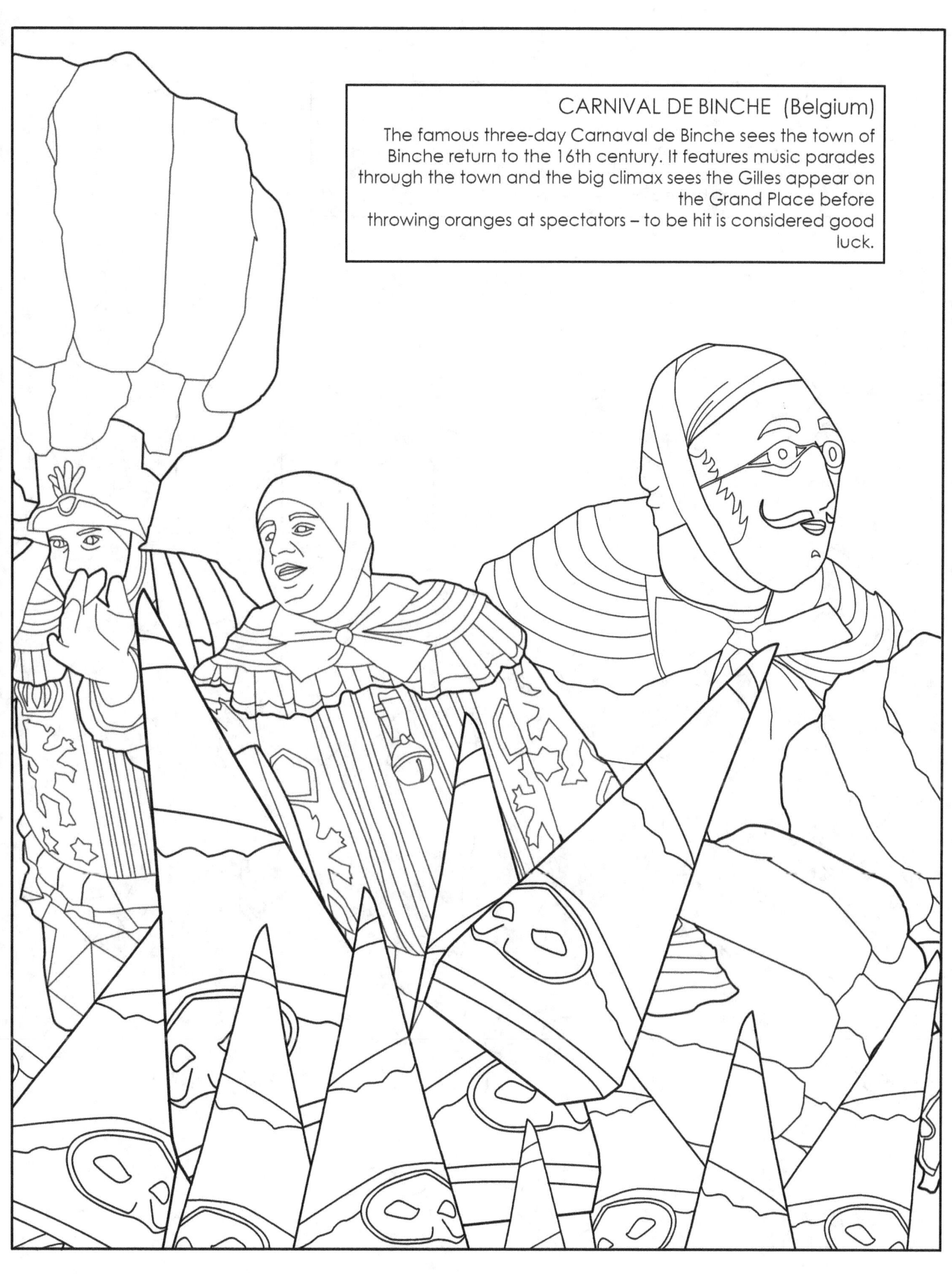

CARNIVAL DE BINCHE (Belgium)
The famous three-day Carnaval de Binche sees the town of Binche return to the 16th century. It features music parades through the town and the big climax sees the Gilles appear on the Grand Place before throwing oranges at spectators – to be hit is considered good luck.

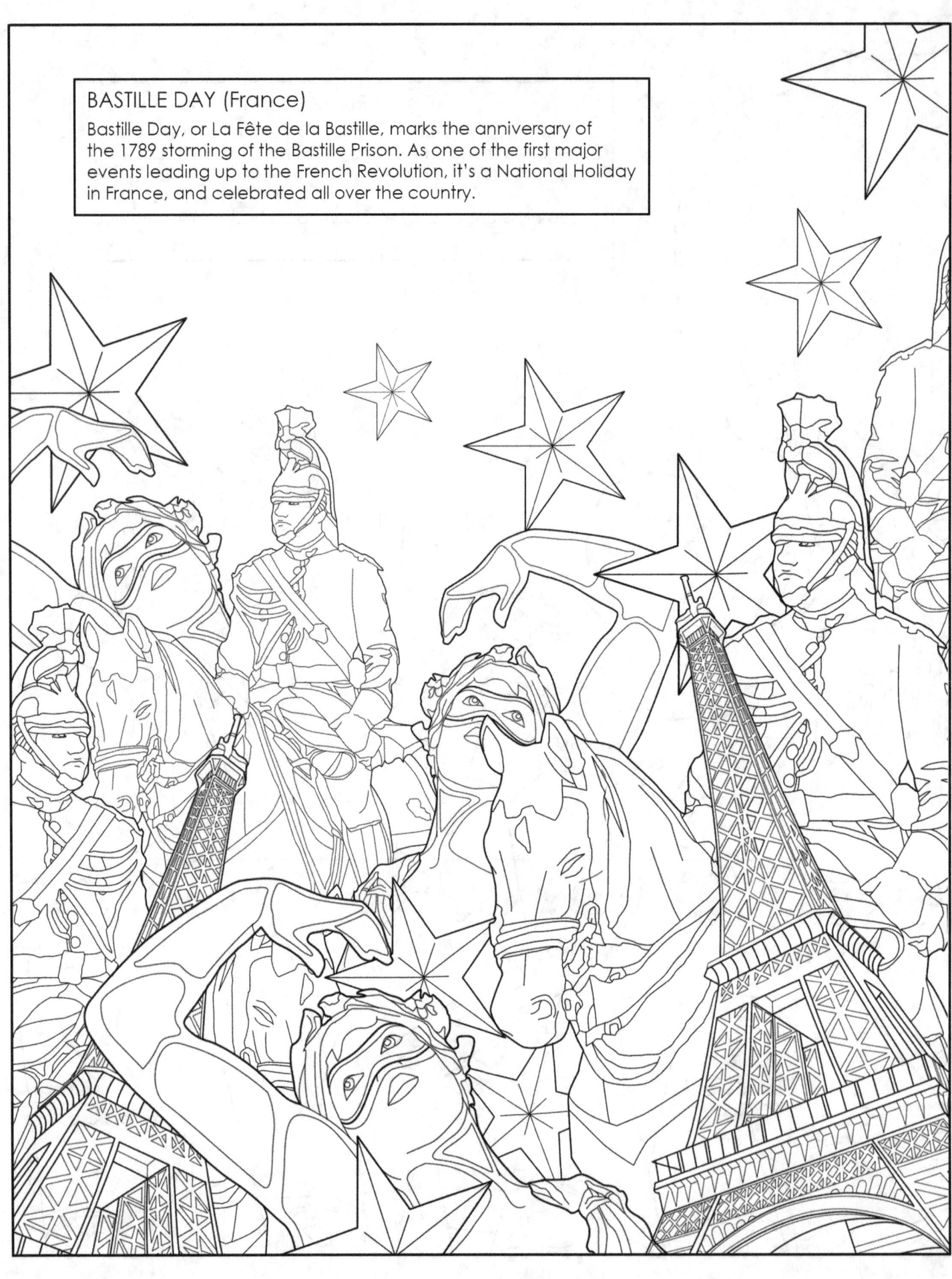

BASTILLE DAY (France)

Bastille Day, or La Fête de la Bastille, marks the anniversary of the 1789 storming of the Bastille Prison. As one of the first major events leading up to the French Revolution, it's a National Holiday in France, and celebrated all over the country.

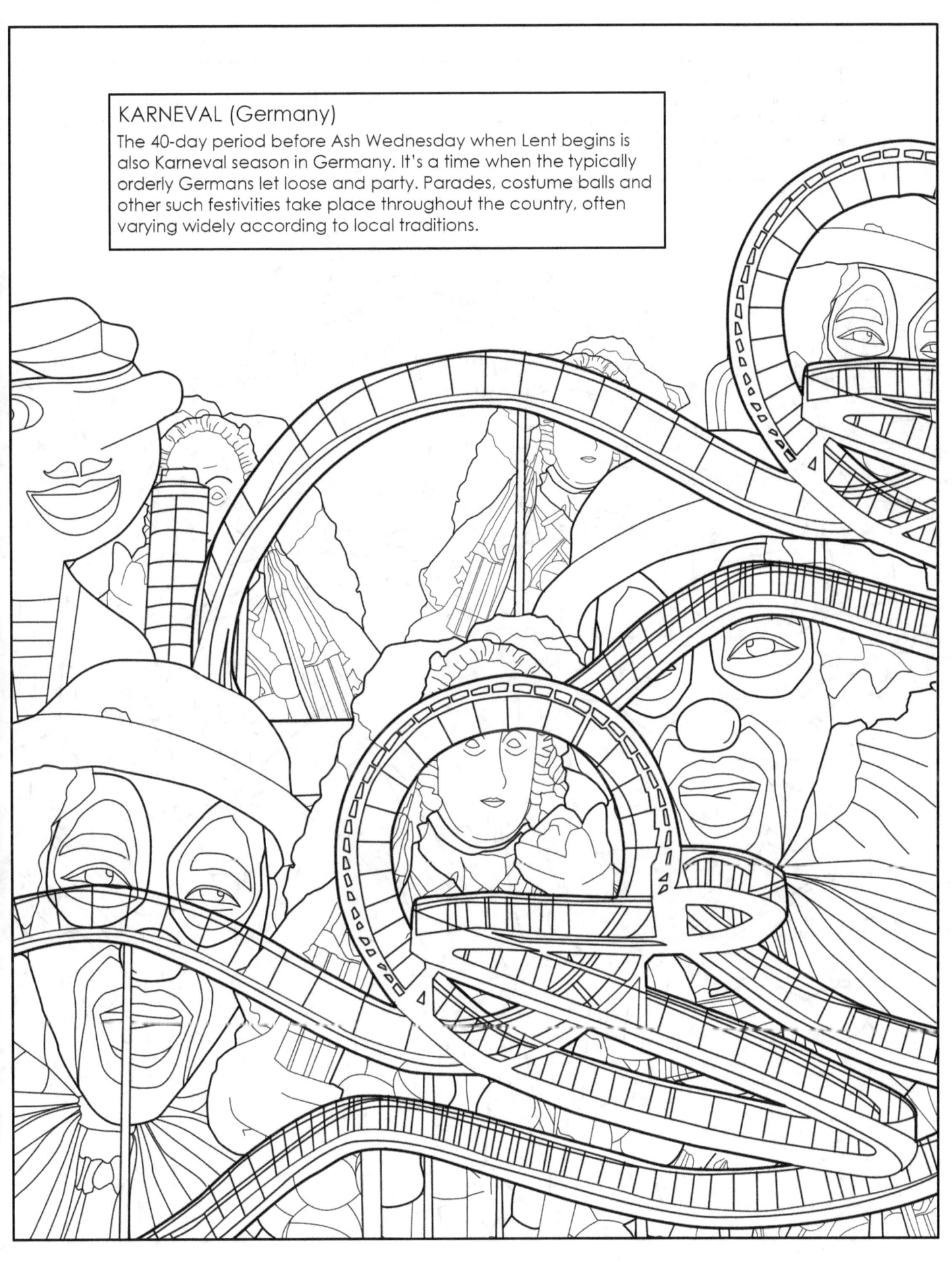

KARNEVAL (Germany)
The 40-day period before Ash Wednesday when Lent begins is also Karneval season in Germany. It's a time when the typically orderly Germans let loose and party. Parades, costume balls and other such festivities take place throughout the country, often varying widely according to local traditions.

OKTOBERFEST (Germany)
Held annually in Munich, Bavaria, Germany, it is a 16- to 18-day folk festival running from mid or late September to the first weekend in October, with more than 6 million people from around the world attending the event every year.
The Oktoberfest is an important part of Bavarian culture, having been held since 1810.

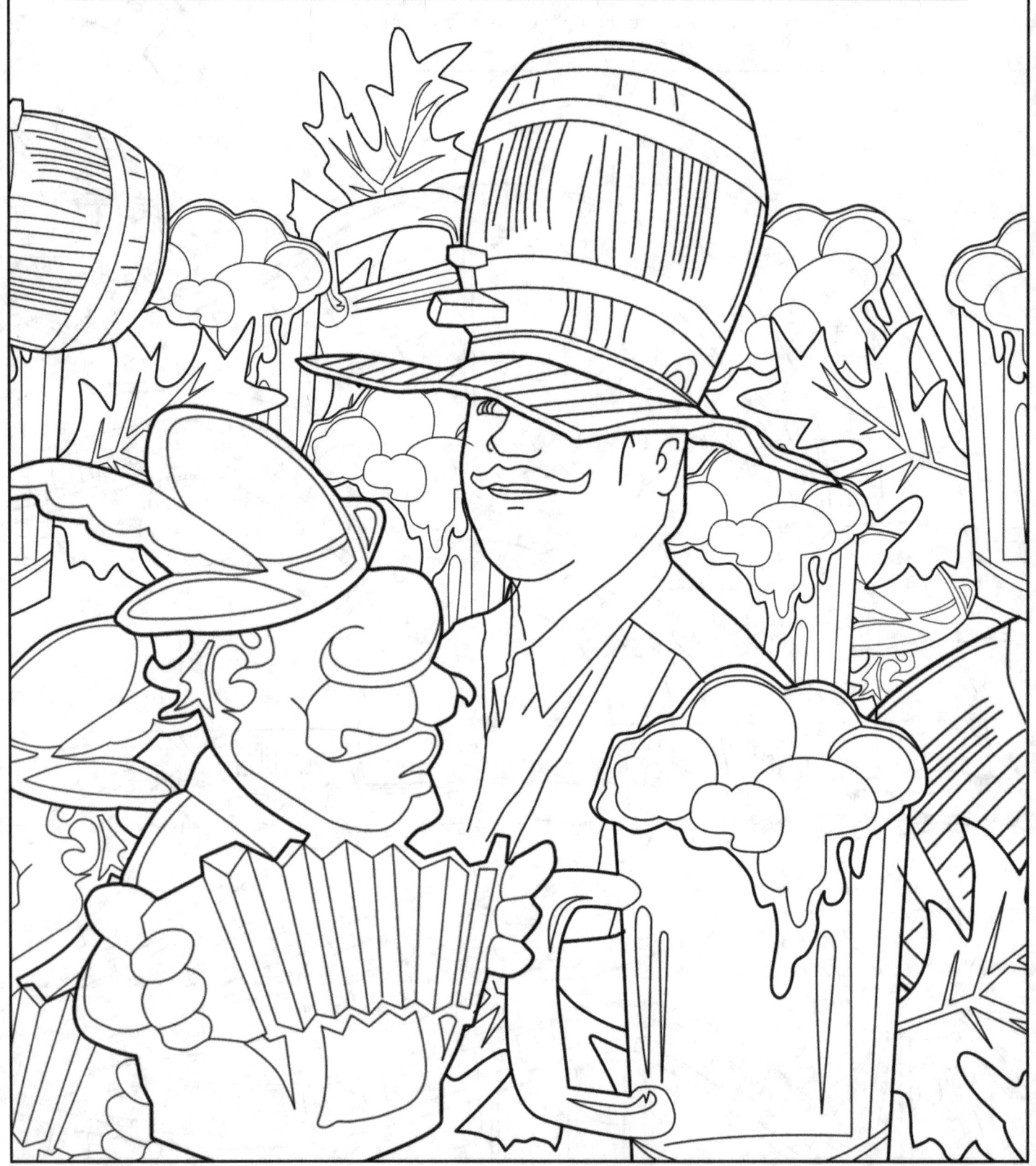

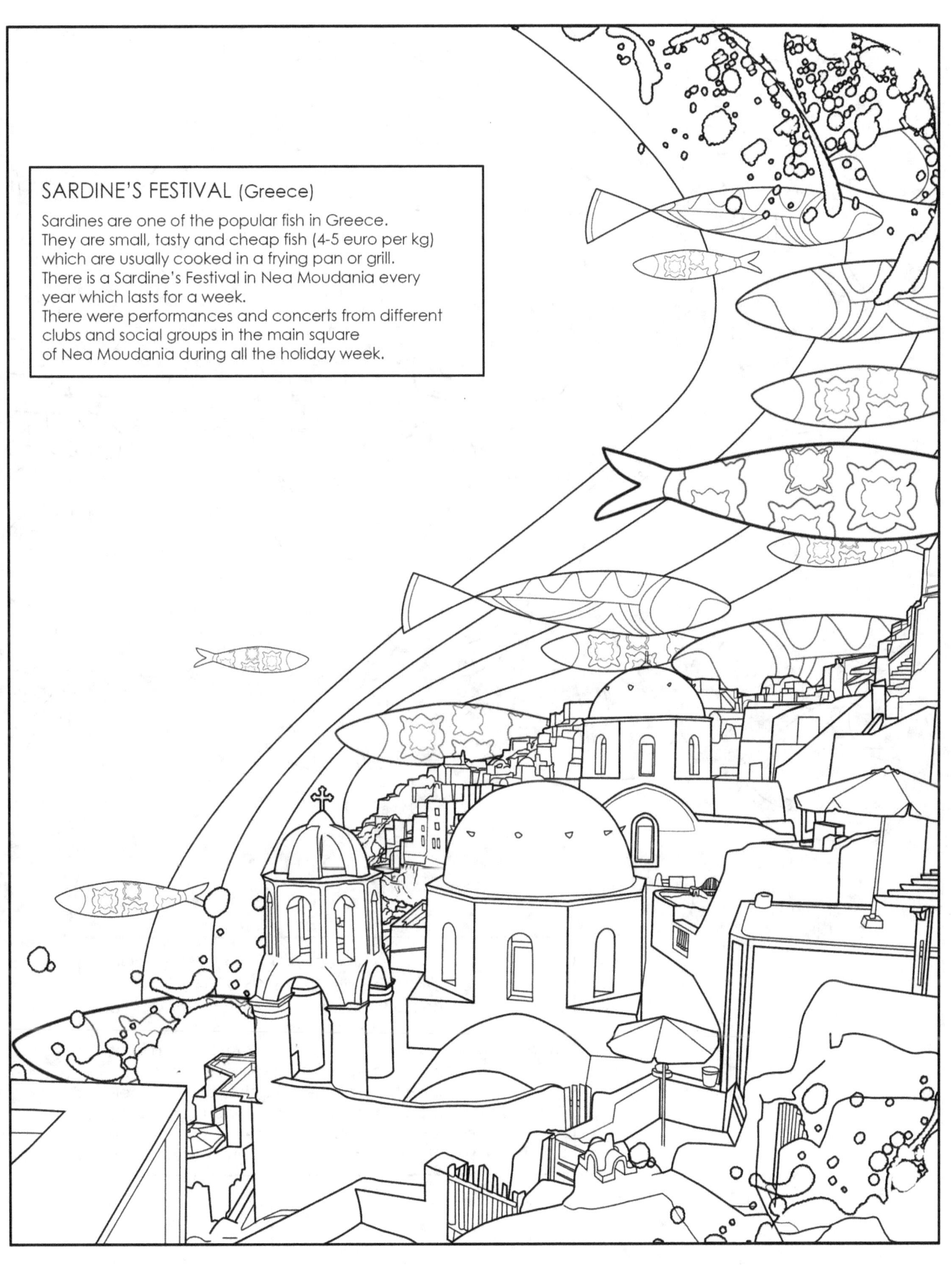

SARDINE'S FESTIVAL (Greece)

Sardines are one of the popular fish in Greece.
They are small, tasty and cheap fish (4-5 euro per kg)
which are usually cooked in a frying pan or grill.
There is a Sardine's Festival in Nea Moudania every
year which lasts for a week.
There were performances and concerts from different
clubs and social groups in the main square
of Nea Moudania during all the holiday week.

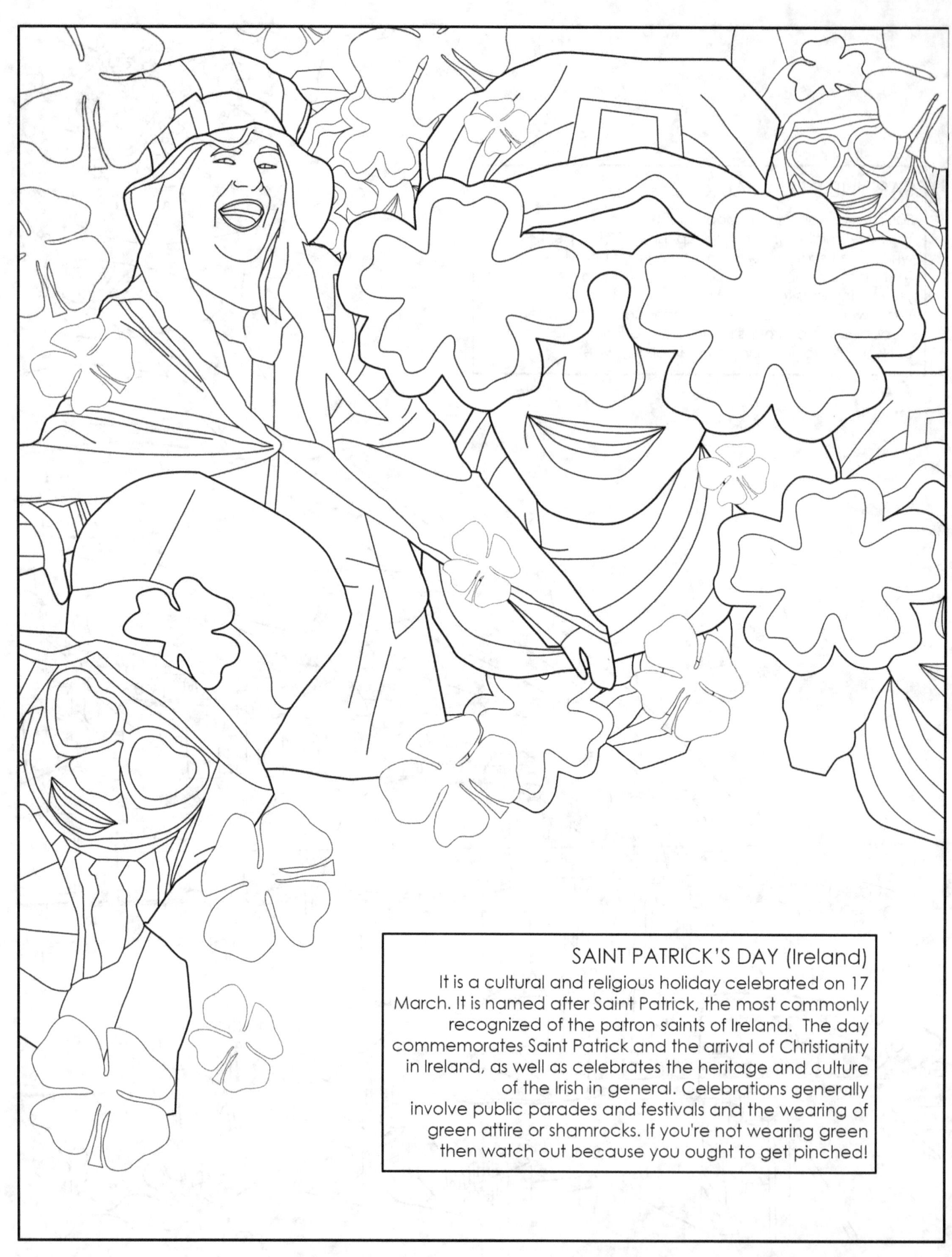

SAINT PATRICK'S DAY (Ireland)
It is a cultural and religious holiday celebrated on 17 March. It is named after Saint Patrick, the most commonly recognized of the patron saints of Ireland. The day commemorates Saint Patrick and the arrival of Christianity in Ireland, as well as celebrates the heritage and culture of the Irish in general. Celebrations generally involve public parades and festivals and the wearing of green attire or shamrocks. If you're not wearing green then watch out because you ought to get pinched!

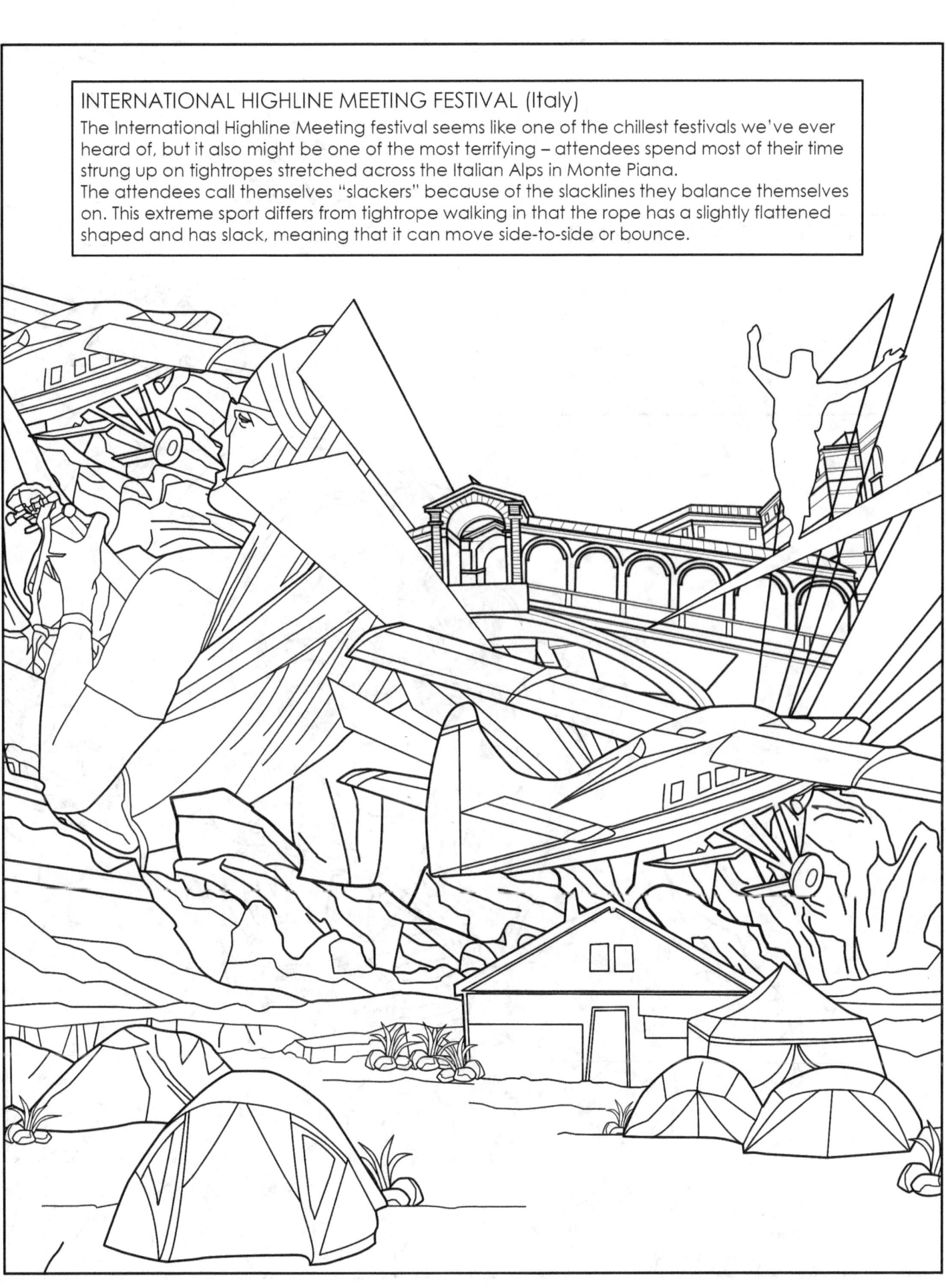

INTERNATIONAL HIGHLINE MEETING FESTIVAL (Italy)

The International Highline Meeting festival seems like one of the chillest festivals we've ever heard of, but it also might be one of the most terrifying – attendees spend most of their time strung up on tightropes stretched across the Italian Alps in Monte Piana.

The attendees call themselves "slackers" because of the slacklines they balance themselves on. This extreme sport differs from tightrope walking in that the rope has a slightly flattened shaped and has slack, meaning that it can move side-to-side or bounce.

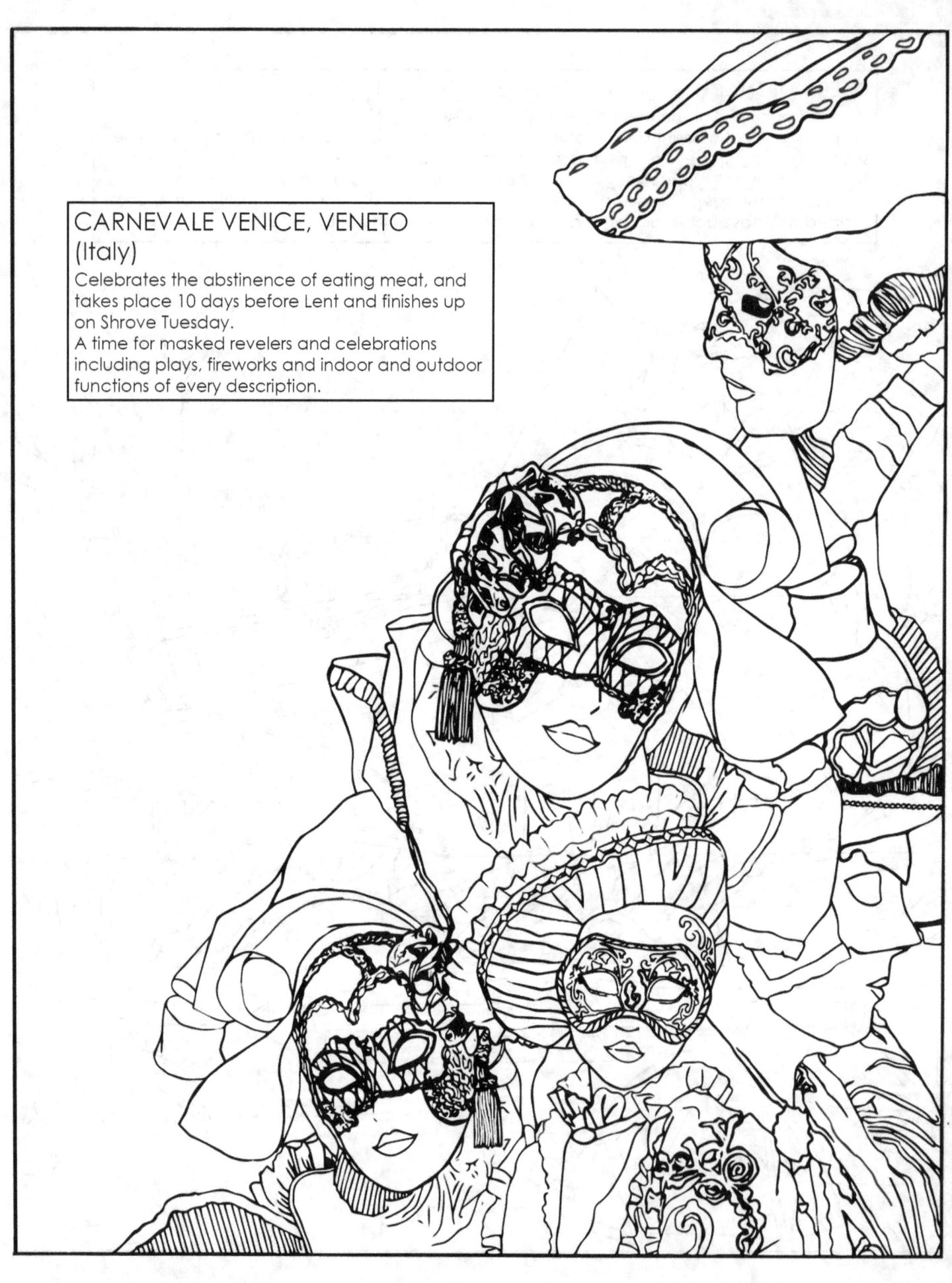

CARNEVALE VENICE, VENETO
(Italy)
Celebrates the abstinence of eating meat, and takes place 10 days before Lent and finishes up on Shrove Tuesday.
A time for masked revelers and celebrations including plays, fireworks and indoor and outdoor functions of every description.

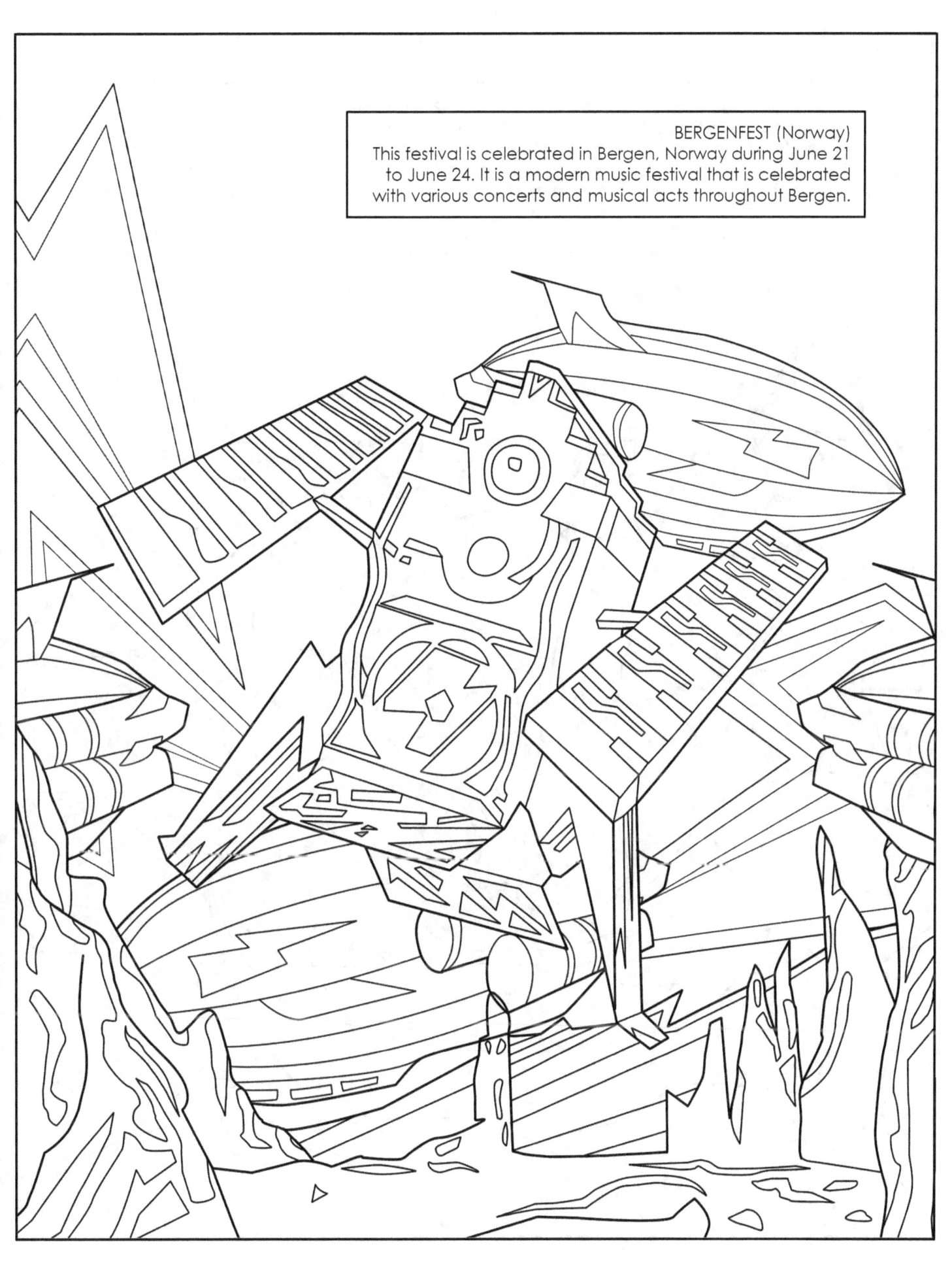

BERGENFEST (Norway)
This festival is celebrated in Bergen, Norway during June 21 to June 24. It is a modern music festival that is celebrated with various concerts and musical acts throughout Bergen.

Ágitagueda art festival in Portugal is not a very old ritual that the festival has witnessed which itself is a very old festival. This practice to hang vibrant, colorful umbrellas started 3 years back. Portugal that is famous for football and food is also home to this wonderful practice. So if you ever visit this majestic place, try to stop by this place during July and get the best view of the vibrant colorful umbrellas. This is one of the best places to visit in Portugal, especially if you are visiting the place in July. The photographers have done an amazing work.

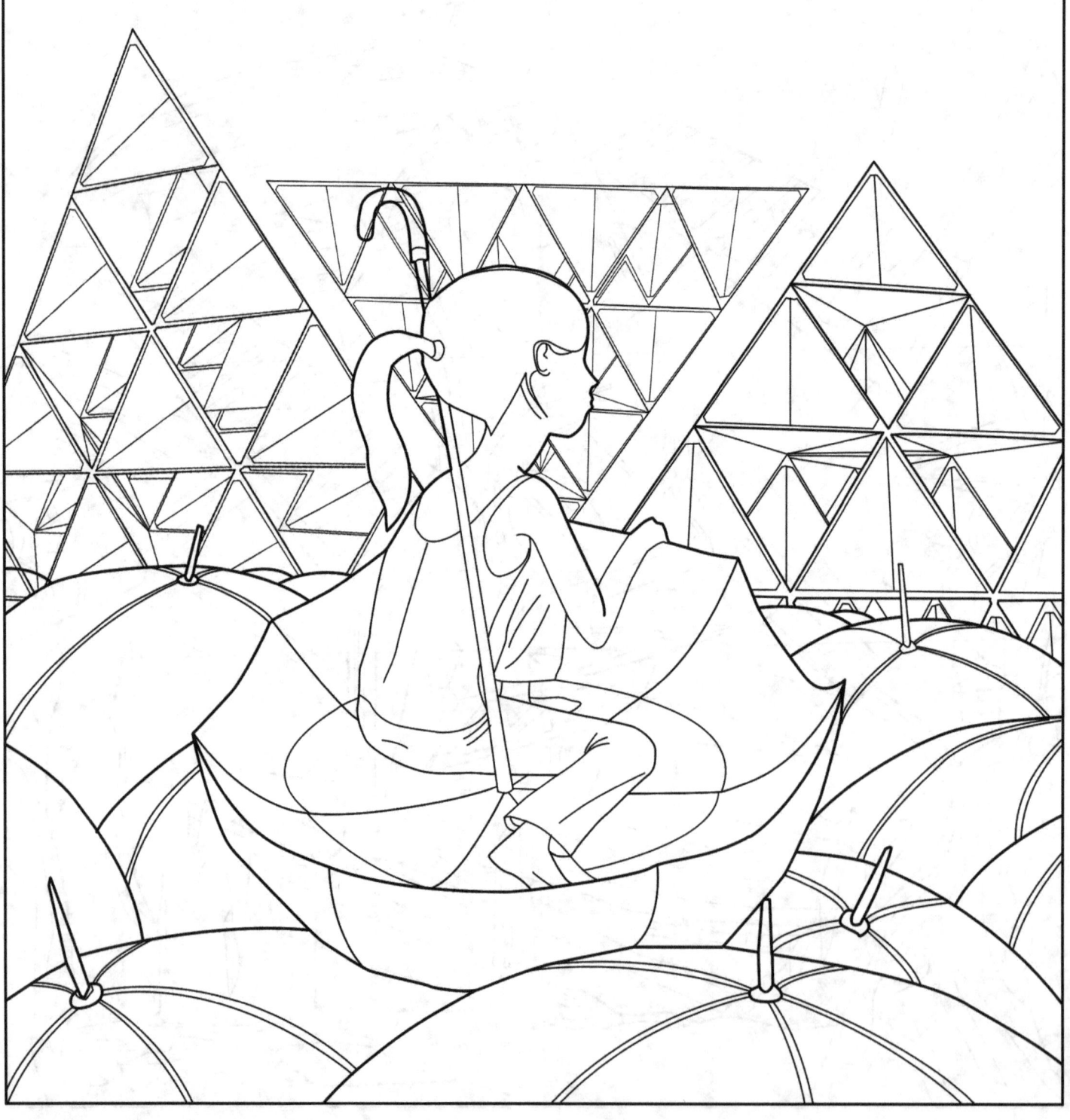

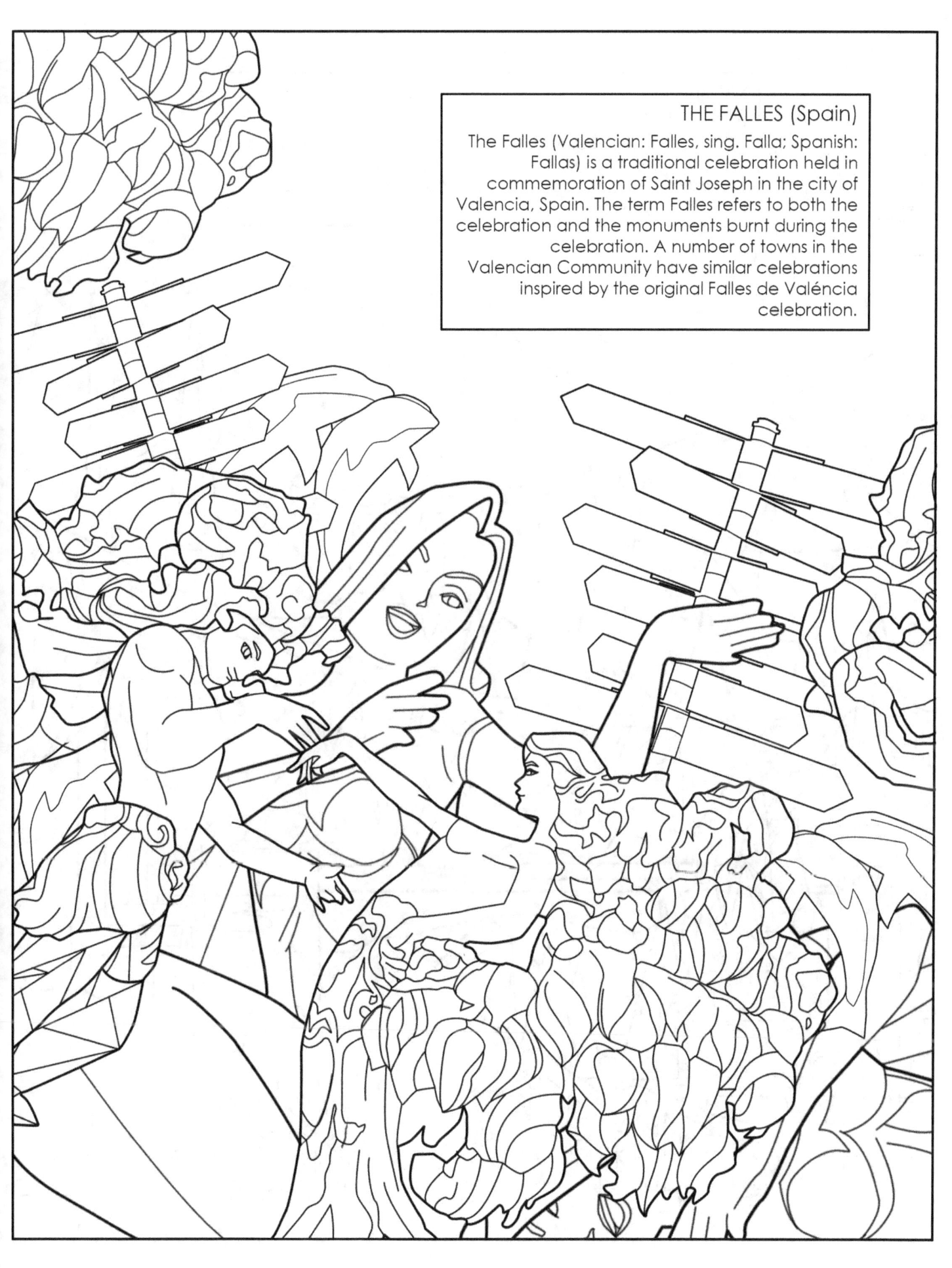

THE FALLES (Spain)

The Falles (Valencian: Falles, sing. Falla; Spanish: Fallas) is a traditional celebration held in commemoration of Saint Joseph in the city of Valencia, Spain. The term Falles refers to both the celebration and the monuments burnt during the celebration. A number of towns in the Valencian Community have similar celebrations inspired by the original Falles de Valéncia celebration.

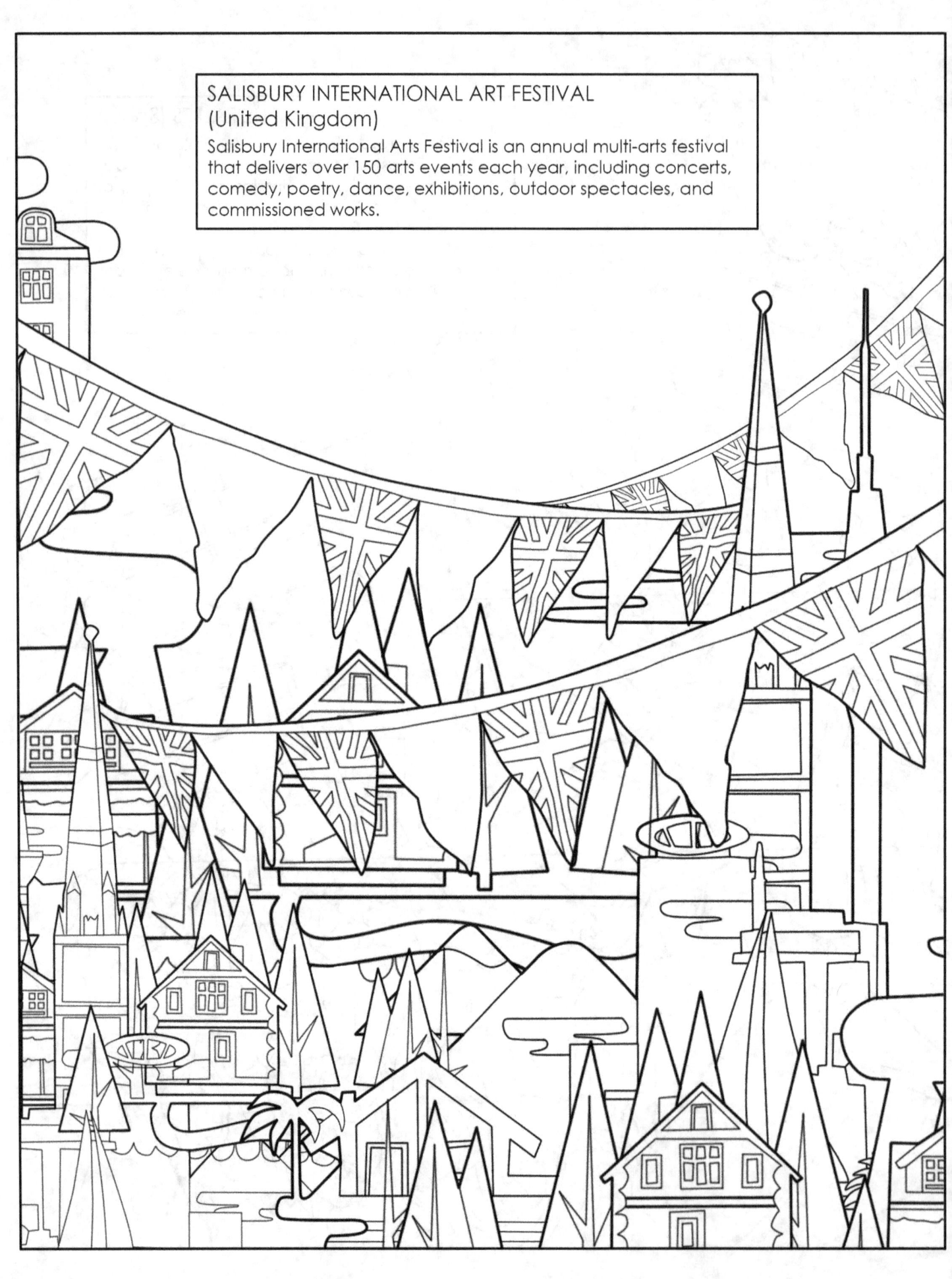

SALISBURY INTERNATIONAL ART FESTIVAL
(United Kingdom)
Salisbury International Arts Festival is an annual multi-arts festival that delivers over 150 arts events each year, including concerts, comedy, poetry, dance, exhibitions, outdoor spectacles, and commissioned works.

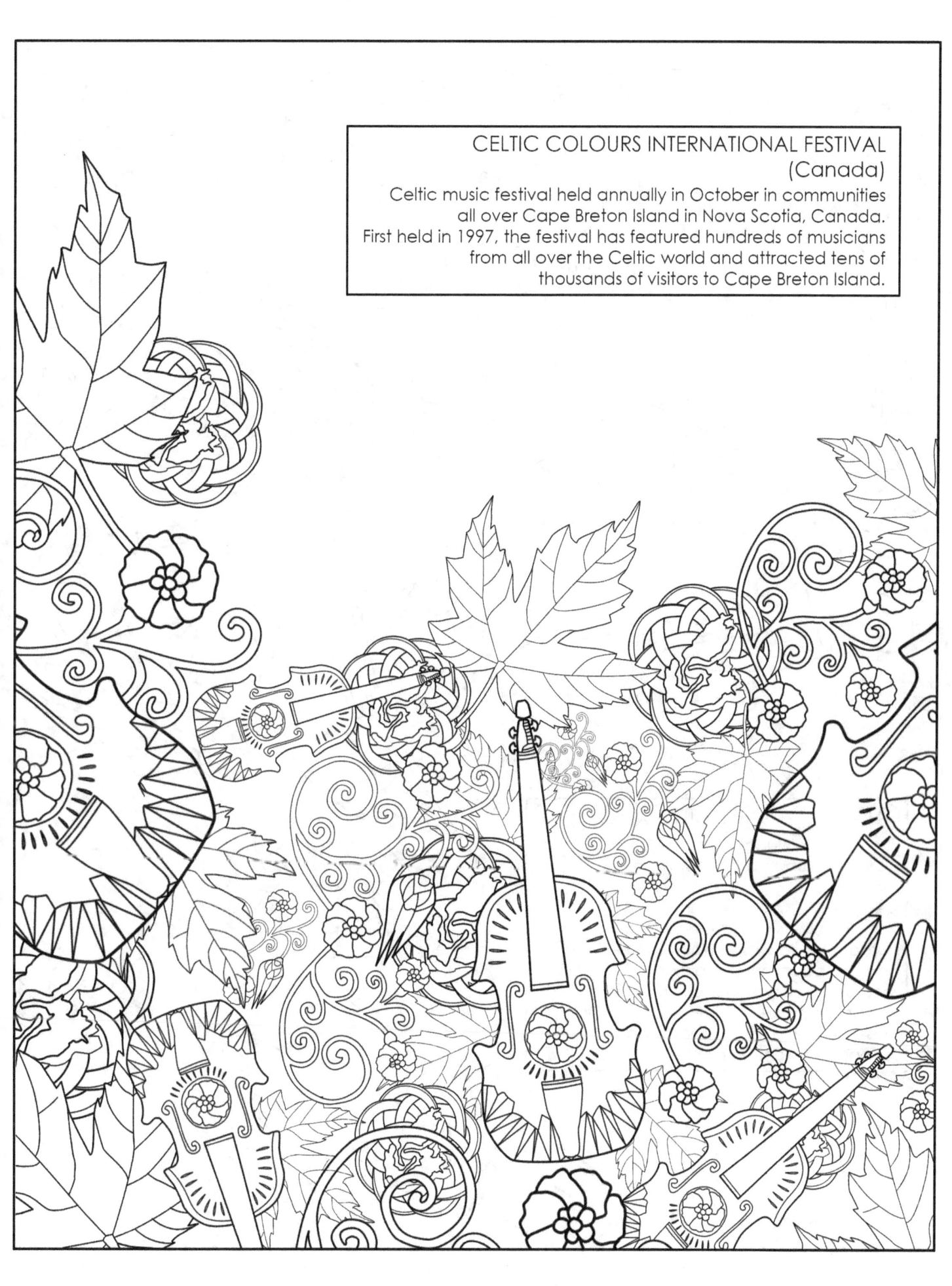

CELTIC COLOURS INTERNATIONAL FESTIVAL
(Canada)
Celtic music festival held annually in October in communities
all over Cape Breton Island in Nova Scotia, Canada.
First held in 1997, the festival has featured hundreds of musicians
from all over the Celtic world and attracted tens of
thousands of visitors to Cape Breton Island.

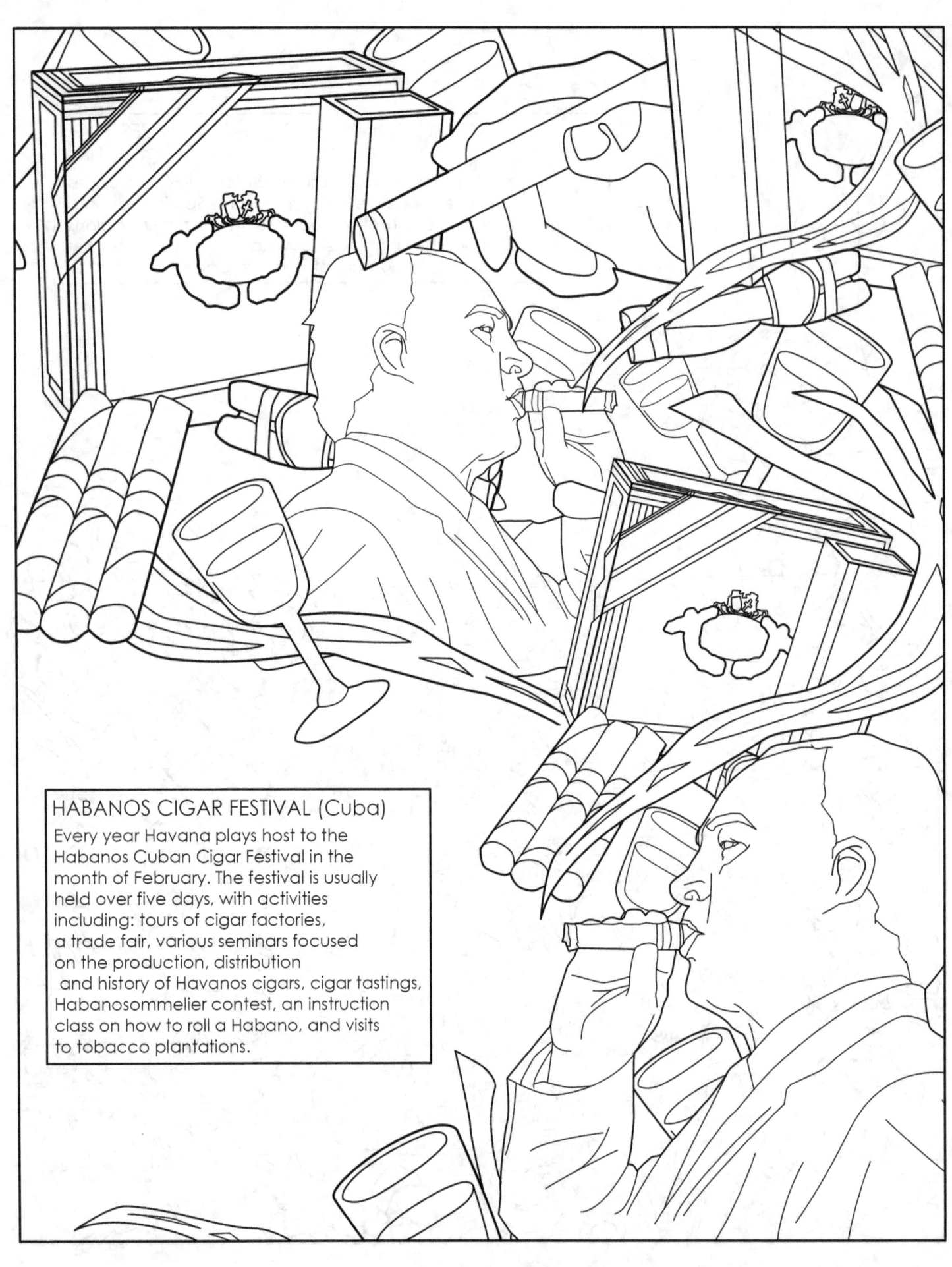

HABANOS CIGAR FESTIVAL (Cuba)
Every year Havana plays host to the
Habanos Cuban Cigar Festival in the
month of February. The festival is usually
held over five days, with activities
including: tours of cigar factories,
a trade fair, various seminars focused
on the production, distribution
and history of Havanos cigars, cigar tastings,
Habanosommelier contest, an instruction
class on how to roll a Habano, and visits
to tobacco plantations.

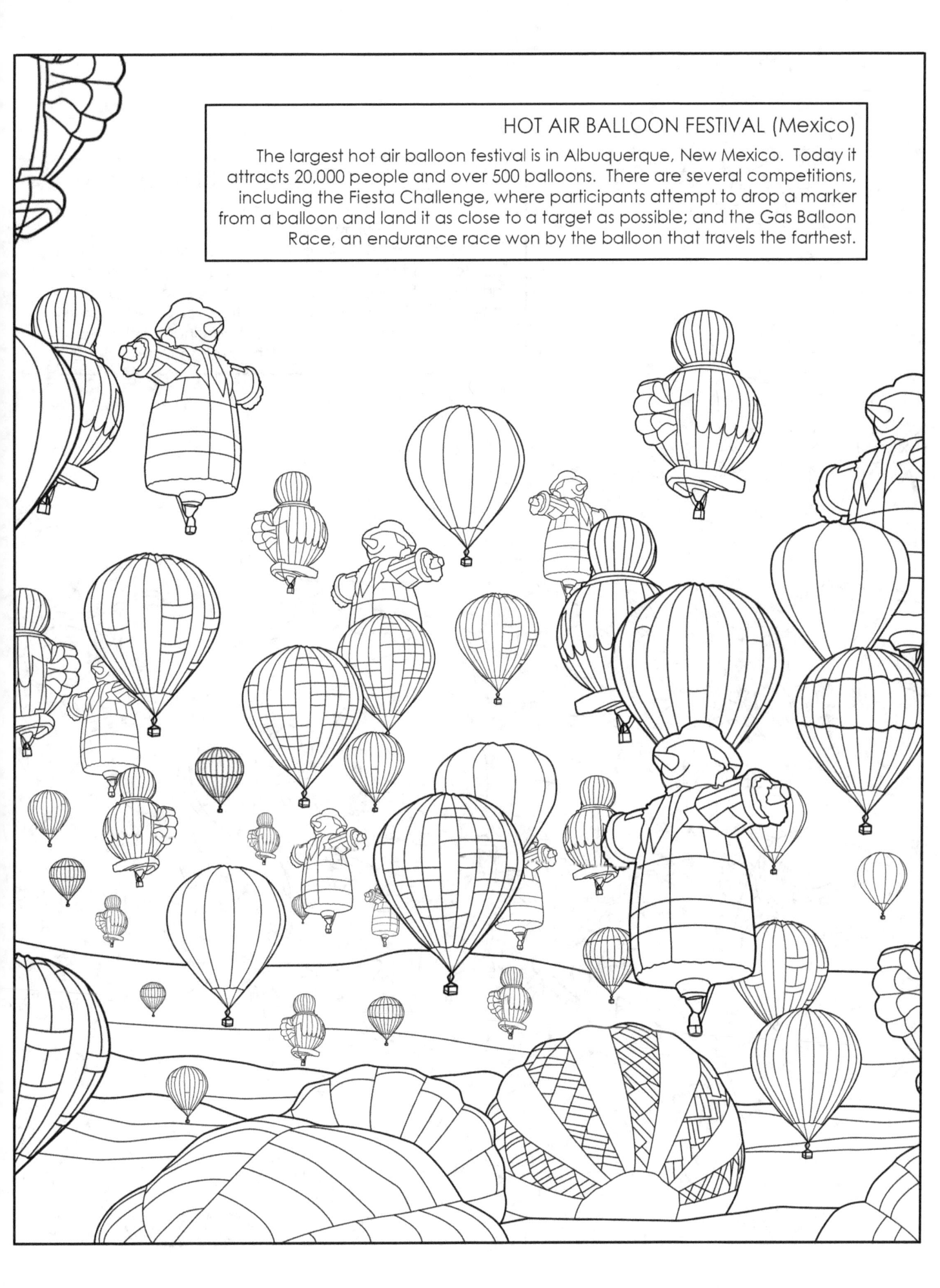

HOT AIR BALLOON FESTIVAL (Mexico)

The largest hot air balloon festival is in Albuquerque, New Mexico. Today it attracts 20,000 people and over 500 balloons. There are several competitions, including the Fiesta Challenge, where participants attempt to drop a marker from a balloon and land it as close to a target as possible; and the Gas Balloon Race, an endurance race won by the balloon that travels the farthest.

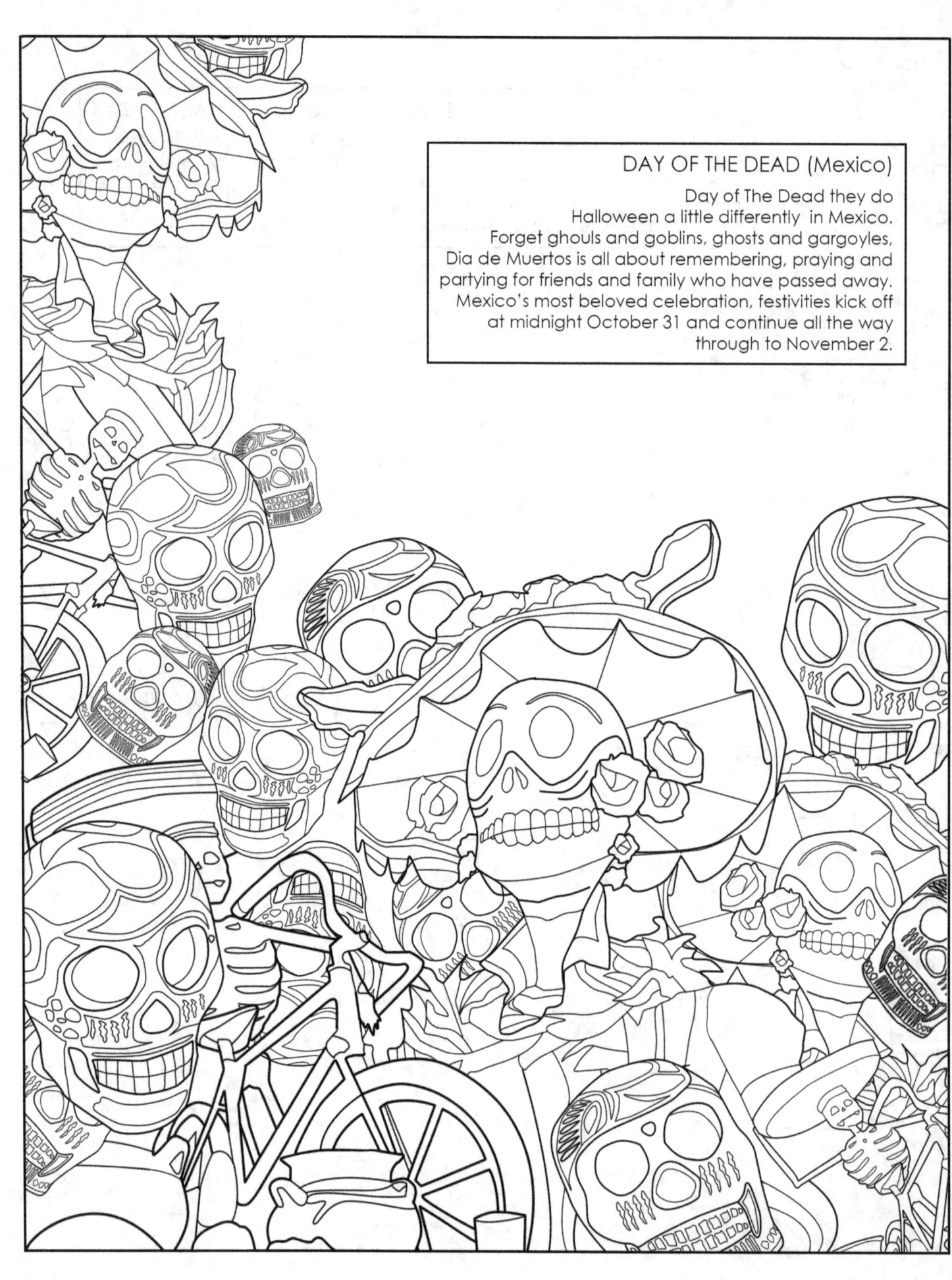

DAY OF THE DEAD (Mexico)

Day of The Dead they do
Halloween a little differently in Mexico.
Forget ghouls and goblins, ghosts and gargoyles,
Dia de Muertos is all about remembering, praying and
partying for friends and family who have passed away.
Mexico's most beloved celebration, festivities kick off
at midnight October 31 and continue all the way
through to November 2.

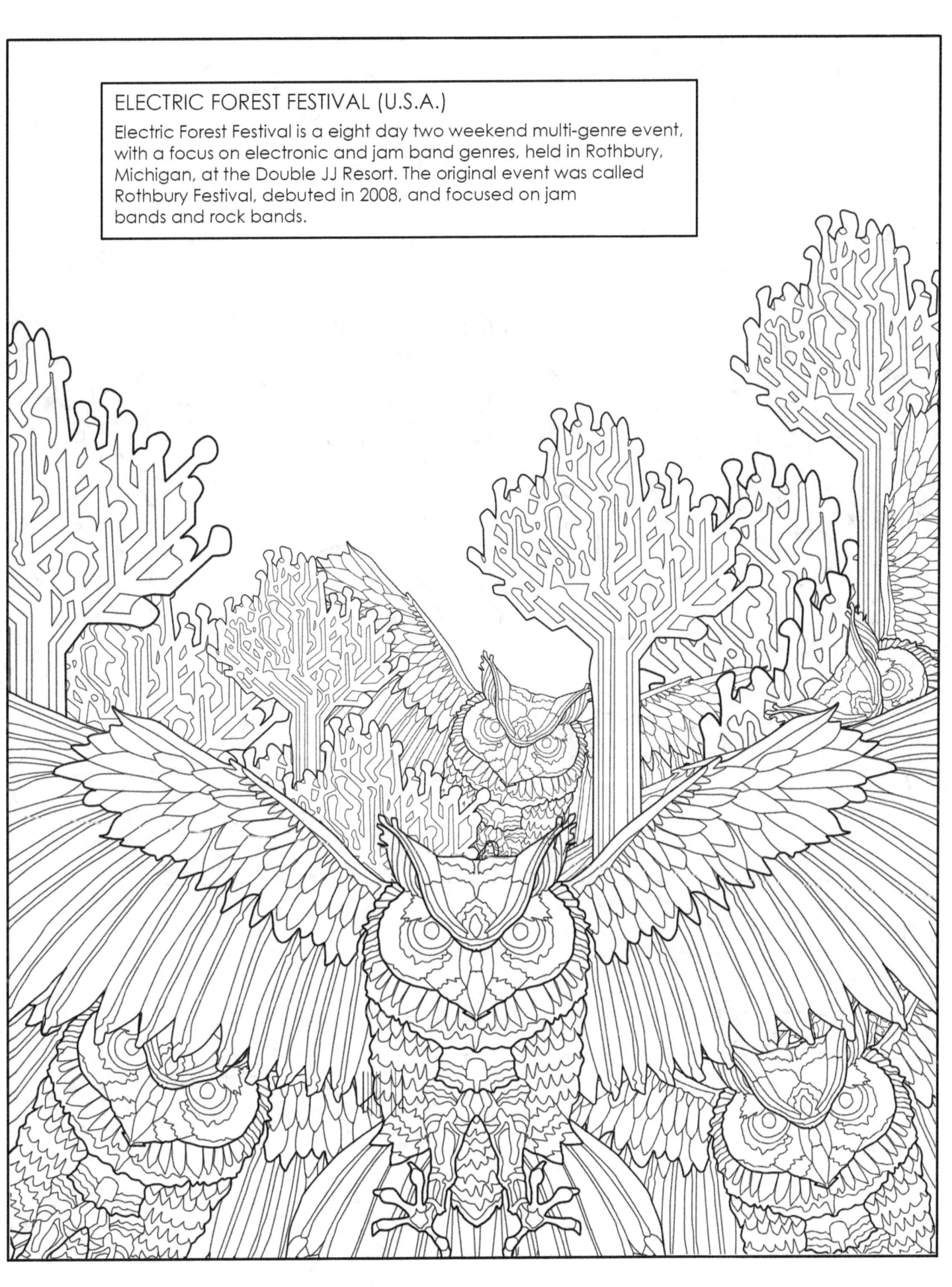

ELECTRIC FOREST FESTIVAL (U.S.A.)
Electric Forest Festival is a eight day two weekend multi-genre event, with a focus on electronic and jam band genres, held in Rothbury, Michigan, at the Double JJ Resort. The original event was called Rothbury Festival, debuted in 2008, and focused on jam bands and rock bands.

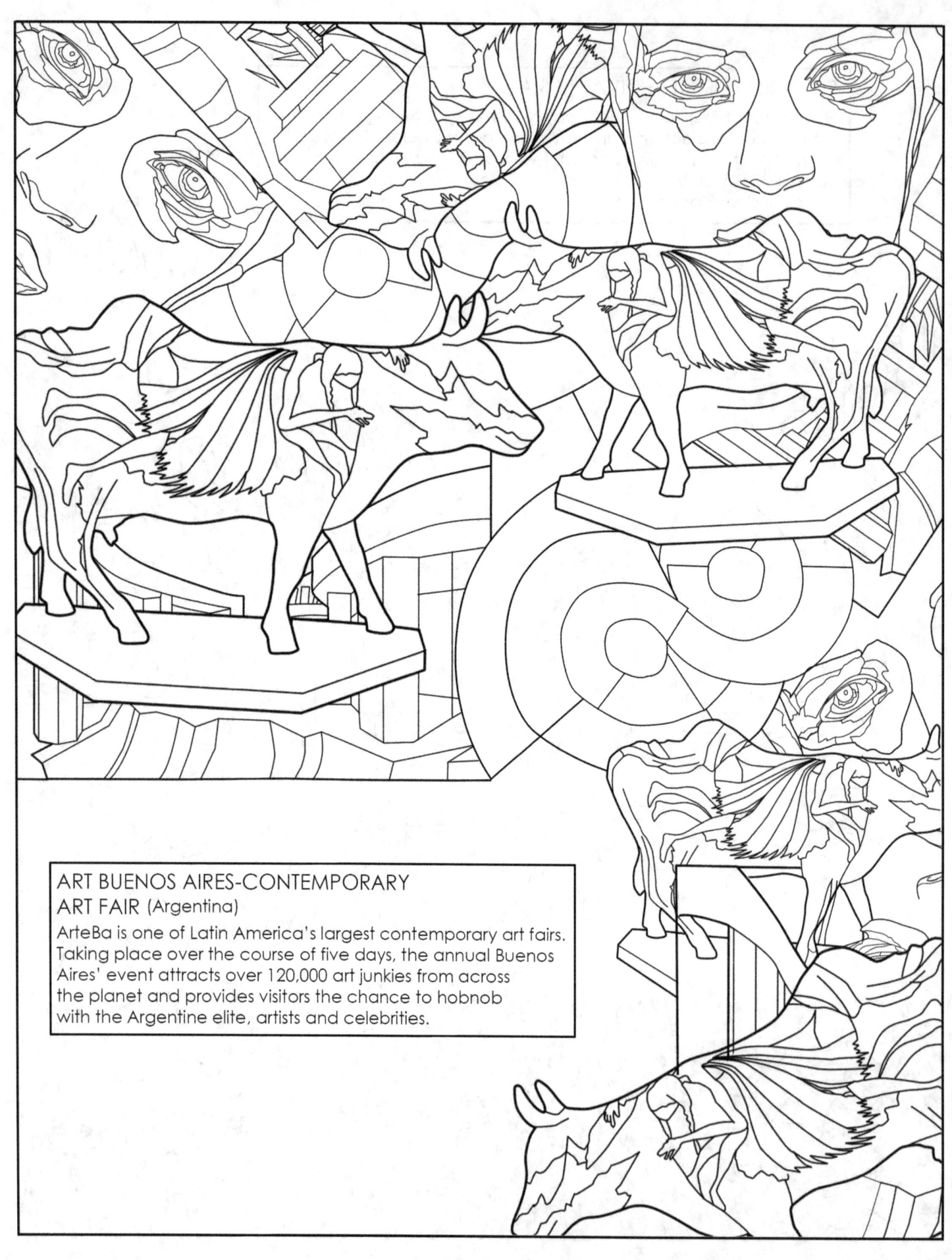

ART BUENOS AIRES-CONTEMPORARY
ART FAIR (Argentina)

ArteBa is one of Latin America's largest contemporary art fairs.
Taking place over the course of five days, the annual Buenos
Aires' event attracts over 120,000 art junkies from across
the planet and provides visitors the chance to hobnob
with the Argentine elite, artists and celebrities.

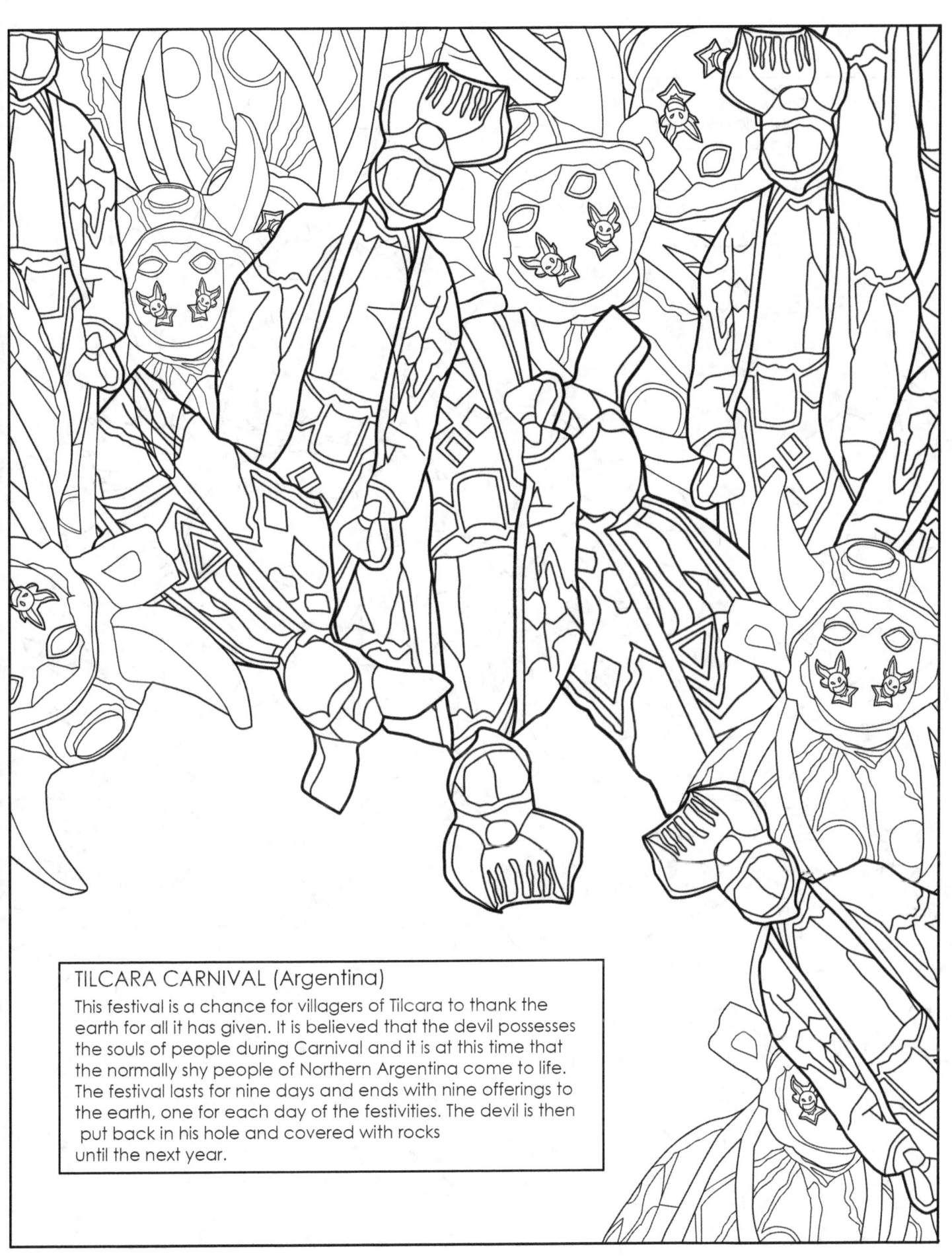

TILCARA CARNIVAL (Argentina)

This festival is a chance for villagers of Tilcara to thank the earth for all it has given. It is believed that the devil possesses the souls of people during Carnival and it is at this time that the normally shy people of Northern Argentina come to life. The festival lasts for nine days and ends with nine offerings to the earth, one for each day of the festivities. The devil is then put back in his hole and covered with rocks until the next year.

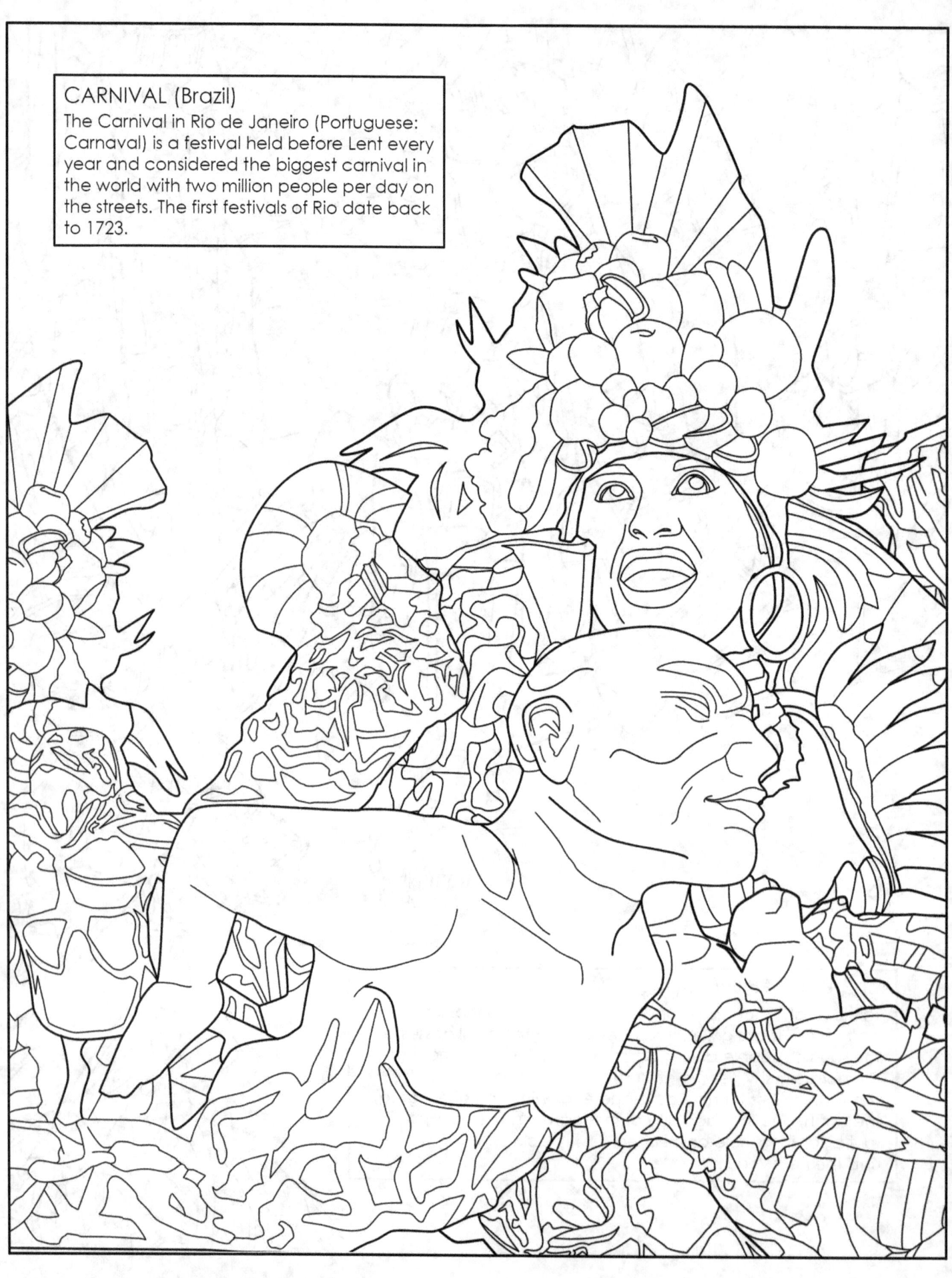

CARNIVAL (Brazil)
The Carnival in Rio de Janeiro (Portuguese: Carnaval) is a festival held before Lent every year and considered the biggest carnival in the world with two million people per day on the streets. The first festivals of Rio date back to 1723.

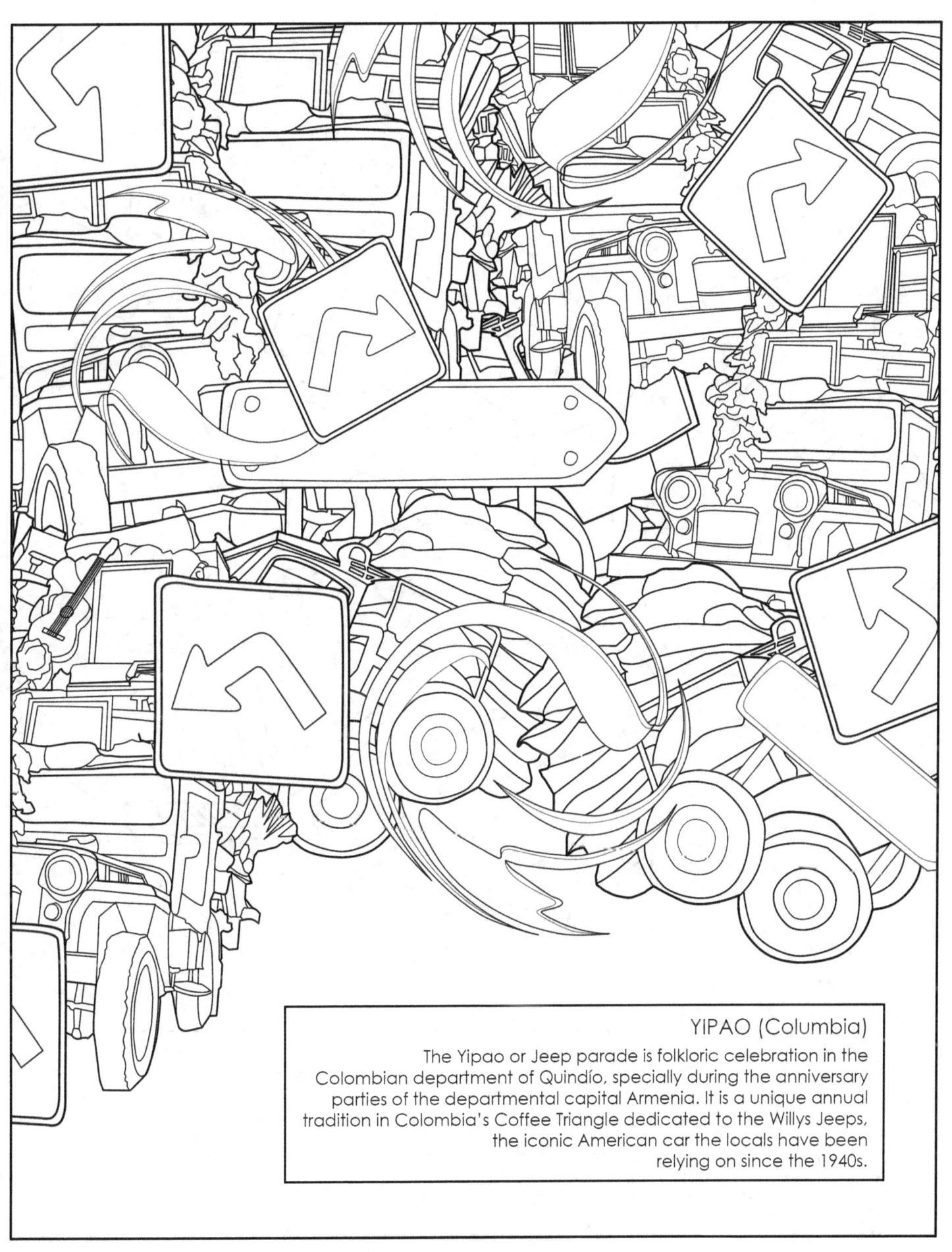

YIPAO (Columbia)

The Yipao or Jeep parade is folkloric celebration in the Colombian department of Quindío, specially during the anniversary parties of the departmental capital Armenia. It is a unique annual tradition in Colombia's Coffee Triangle dedicated to the Willys Jeeps, the iconic American car the locals have been relying on since the 1940s.

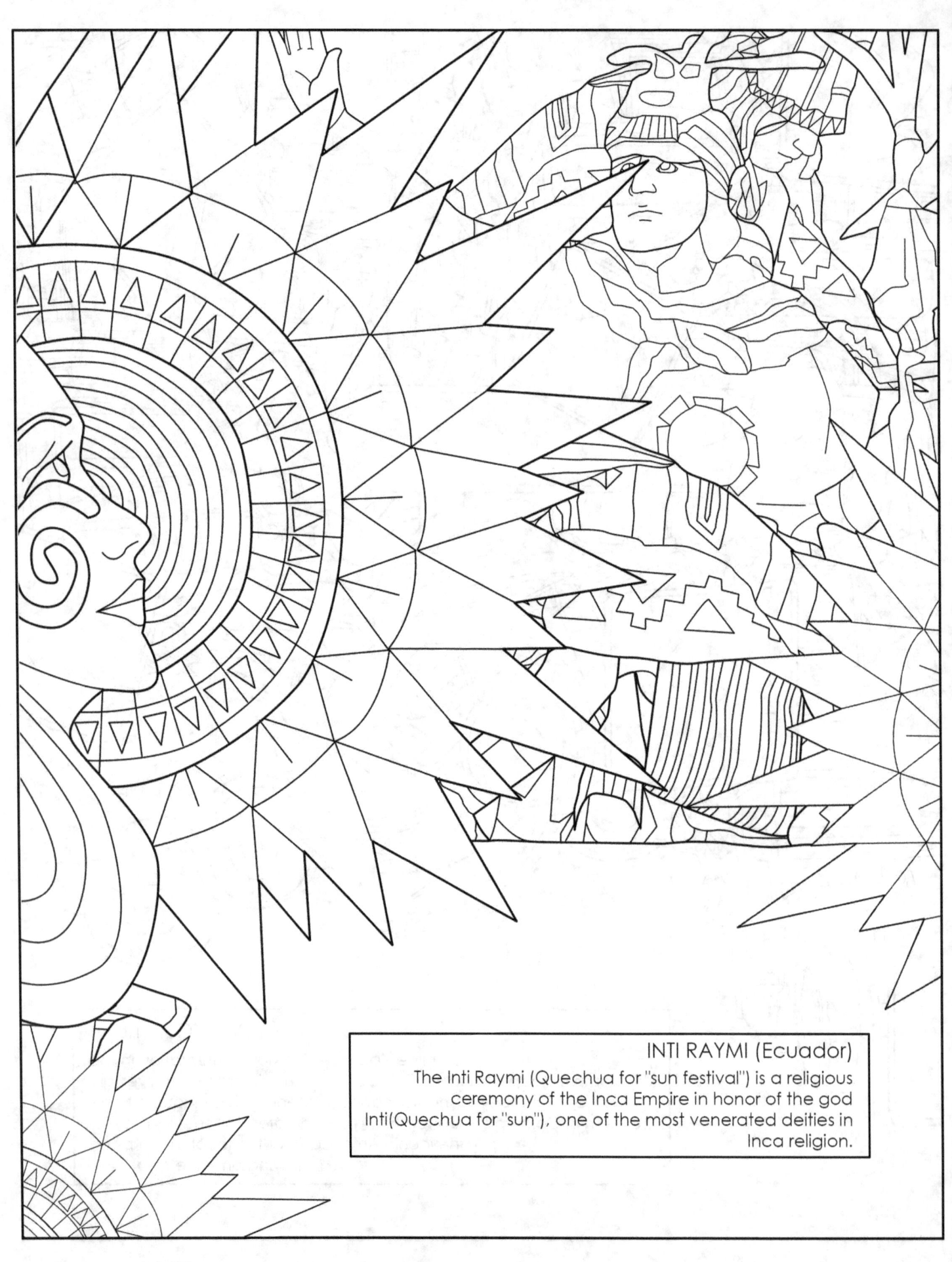

INTI RAYMI (Ecuador)
The Inti Raymi (Quechua for "sun festival") is a religious
ceremony of the Inca Empire in honor of the god
Inti(Quechua for "sun"), one of the most venerated deities in
Inca religion.